A North Country Life

A North Country Life

Tales of Woodsmen, Waters, and Wildlife

by Sydney Lea

Skyhorse Publishing

The author and publisher gratefully acknowledge the permission granted to reproduce the copyright material in this book. Every effort has been made to trace copyright holders and to obtain their permission for the use of the material herein. If there are any inadvertent omissions we apologize to those concerned and would be grateful if notified so that we can amend future reprints or editions of this book.

Lines from the poem "Angina" are reprinted from Recounting the Seasons: Collected Poems, 1958–2003 (2005) by John Engels with permission of the University of Notre Dame Press.

Skyhorse Publishing books may be purchased in bulk at special discounts for sales promotion, corporate gifts, fund-raising, or educational purposes. Special editions can also be created to specifications. For details, contact the Special Sales Department, Skyhorse Publishing, 307 West 36th Street, 11th Floor, New York, NY 10018 or info@skyhorsepublishing.com.

Skyhorse® and Skyhorse Publishing® are registered trademarks of Skyhorse Publishing, Inc.®, a Delaware corporation.

www.skyhorsepublishing.com

10 9 8 7 6 5 4 3 2 1

Library of Congress Cataloging-in-Publication Data
Lea, Sydney, 1942-
A north country life : tales of woodsmen, waters, and wildlife / by Sydney Lea.
    p. cm.
Summary: "A collection of essays, organized by the changing of the seasons, about the author's strong connection to his family, friends, and the northern outdoors"–Provided by publisher.
ISBN 978-1-61608-863-7 (hardcover : alk. paper)
1. Outdoor life. I. Title.
PS3562.E16N67 2013
814'.54–dc23
          2012034517

Printed in the United States of America

For all the great old teachers of whom I speak here, as I will everywhere, all the days of my life, and for David Tobey, living heir.

Contents

FOREWORD	ix
ACKNOWLEDGMENTS	xi
PRELUDE	xiii
COLD TIME	1
Weathers and Places	3
Daybook, February	12
That Little Boy You're Holding	13
Daybook, March	21
SPRING	23
Dirt and Blossom	25
Daybook, Mid-April	28
Now Look	29
The Turkey Cure	39
Daybook, May	47
Ownership	49
Daybook, June	56
Appetite	57
SUMMER	65
The Crossing	67
Brown, Gilbey's, Happy Ending	70
Daybook, July	76

Living with the Stories   81

Small Wonders   96

    Daybook, August   105

Everything Comes Together   106

FALL   113

    Daybook, Late September   115

Turned Around   117

Refurbishment   131

    Daybook, October   140

Eighty Percenters: Reflections on Grouse
    and Grouse Dogs   142

Blessed   154

    Daybook, November   165

God Bless Hunting   167

    Daybook, December   176

Trust   178

COLD TIME: REPRISE   189

    Daybook, January   191

Wild Black Duck   193

Snowdust   197

    ABOUT THE AUTHOR   207

Foreword

"It's a changed world," says Earl Bonness, an eighty-eight-year-old former North Country lumberjack and guide. "We told stories. We lived with stories." Sydney Lea's wonderful new book is no idyll of a perfect past, but a vivid and enduring profile of a place and its people and a sure stay against the passing of that older New England world and its towering "barrel-chested, deep-voiced characters." His own stories and tales, journal or "Daybook" entries, poems and essays—full of wit, sharp images, and humanity—let us enter and live in that passing world. Some passages are directly addressed to those great figures, some are given to us in their own earthy words. There is a poignant letter to a father gone, a portrait of a particular bird dog on point, a stunning battle with an outsized trout. Throughout there is an incrementing of the author's rich character—through what he has learned and sees and through his nimble language—so that what may at first seem random builds inexorably to a full and textured story of a man's unique life.

His is a life "addicted to the natural world"—and Lea has grown to know it intimately: the turkey coming out of the "hop horn-beam grove"; the ways of nighthawk, woodcock, grouse, and red-ringed blackbird; the unforgettable sound of two barred owls "yammering." The book is framed by seasons in the North Country, from one "Cold Time" through spring, summer, and fall to another winter. For each, he finds discrete words and emblems with his poet's shrewd eye—"Spring, with its tobacco-and-mushroom odor in the leaf mold," or fall marked by his flushing "a grouse from behind a rootball."

Hunting pervades every aspect of Lea's life. It is the hinge that helps to blend the "natural and human worlds" for him, and his spirited celebration of hunting is marked everywhere by the humanity it breeds, from his love of his dogs to the solitude of the woods in their season; from the great life forces in his mentors and companions to the way in which the entire ritual encourages him to see and experience the natural world more deeply.

Lea's ear, upon which little is lost, is always attuned to the pungent sounds of words, the names of things special to his North Country—places with names like Slewgundy Ridge, Big Musquash Stream, Freeze-to-Death Island, Slaughter Point. He is attached to each of his bird dogs, Hector, Gus, Sam, Bessie, Pete, and others, but mostly he treasures the great presences of his great teachers, many of them gone, to make them "a part of today." They are men and women educated by the earth and by their often hard lives, who knew forest and river, who had diverse and finely tuned skills, who never shied from their hardest work, who taught him woodcraft and how to fish and hunt wisely. Like a great wind, elders such as Creston MacArthur and his uncle George, Don Chambers, Mattie, Annie Fitch, Carter White, Bill White, and the irresistible Earl Bonness bring him "back to his senses." But while he savors memories of what has perished, and what remains that he wants to preserve, he refuses elegies, which feel to him "like posture, pretense, artifice."

This book is instead a celebration—of affections, closeness to woods and waters, and images and people who will last. He cannot hold back what is slipping downstream but he can remember and cherish and embody. Always in *A North Country Life,* Sydney Lea looks hard and brilliantly at his unique world, looking for "specific meanings, cryptic but crucial."

—Nick Lyons
Woodstock, New York
October 2012

Acknowledgments

Some of these chapters, frequently in quite different shape and/or under different titles, have appeared in the following periodicals or anthologies, whose editors I thank for their kindness:

Gray's Sporting Journal, "Eighty Percenters: Reflections on Grouse and Grouse Dogs," "God Bless Hunting," "Turned Around," "Wild Black Duck"

Northern Woodlands, "Prelude," "Daybook, December," "Daybook, March," "Daybook, May," "Dirt and Blossom"

Rise Forms, "Brown, Gilbey's, Happy Ending" (online)

Trout, "Daybook, June"

Afield (eds. Dave Smith and Robert DeMott, 2010, Skyhorse Publishing), "Blessed"

Numéro Cinq, "Weathers and Places"

From Daughters & Sons to Fathers: What I've Never Said (ed. Constance Warloe, Story Line Press, 2001), "That Little Boy You're Holding"

River Teeth, "Now Look"

Prairie Schooner, "Living with the Stories: Bonness Verbatim"

The Southern Review, "The Turkey Cure"(also included in *The Gigantic Book of Hunting Stories*, Jay Cassell, ed., Skyhorse Publishing, 2008)

Ascent, "Ownership"

The Georgia Review, "Appetite"

Margie, "Daybook, July"

Note:

In the far greater portion of the pages that follow, despite a foray or two into the Mountain West and the pastoral Pennsylvania of my earliest years, I meditate on somewhat out-of-the-way parts of upper New England: places I've lived in, fished, hunted, and haunted.

The essays chronicle a life, my own (though who has only one life?), in relation to its region and more crucially to a number of the region's inhabitants. I grieve that too many of those friends, who so blessed my life as man and writer, died before I could get to such a project. We shall never see their like again.

I've always been intrigued by the blending of natural and human worlds—or rather by the dramatic *illustration* of that blending, which is after all an abiding one, however we may veil it in our technological era. I commemorate men and women for whom that blending was simply a given, something they never so much as considered. There could be no veil.

I have given aliases to a couple of them, or in some cases made a composite character from several people I knew well. I take these liberties in the first instance because I have little right to explain other human beings' pains and passions *for* them, and in the latter because the strategy strikes me, paradoxically, as providing a surer way to truth than what passes these days for unvarnished memoir.

In short, some of these accounts hover uncertainly between fiction and essay, as I hope I make clear in their presentation. Here and there, having small choice, I've taken a scrap of history passed on to me by this elder or that, and attempted to construct as plausible a story as I could from a mere clue. In such chapters, however, and everywhere, I seek above all the truthful *flavor* of a territory and people, rather than cut-and-dried factuality.

I have models for such an approach among the folks whom I honor here. As the nonpareil lumberjack poet-raconteur George MacArthur once told me, *The Gospel truth ain't the only truth.*

Prelude

Hookum-snuffie. Almost no one knows what it means anymore, and few would care.

Why should they?

More and more, everything about me seems out of date, perhaps to an even greater degree than with most people of a certain age. Not much after dawn today, for instance, I took my ash paddle, fashioned by the late Hazen Bagley, and set out on the water in a sixteen-foot wood and canvas canoe, fabricated by the Old Town Company in 1950.

I inherited the boat from my long-gone father's late brother. The men took their sons far north to this part of Maine in that canoe and its partner, my dad's eighteen-footer, which blew off a beach some years after in a storm, never to be recovered. A mystery, a vanishing, among many. I was nine years old on that first trip.

Those guide model canoes were more than merely beautiful. The hull planks were feathered, not butted, for example, to keep sand and grit out of their seams. The fabled Grand Lake Stream canoe-maker, Lawrence "Pop" Moore, told me he considered them among the best such craft ever produced.

An hour and some back, my canoe glided me, its progress as smooth as the lake itself, to the foot of the Machias River at Third Lake Dam.

To one like me, of course, there is far more complex and inscrutable technology at work nowadays than ever went into a canoe, no matter how exquisitely made. What can it mean, even out here, to be such a paddler in an era of jet skis? Perhaps more daunting, at least to me, what is a writer in an age of Internet service even at the summit of Mt. Everest?

Twitter. Google. Facebook. Skype.

What does solitude signify anymore? What on earth is a poet, not to mention a poet-woodsman, poet-angler, poet-hunter? Will he have any readers at all? If so, this is for them, though it's even more for each of the men and women I'll be conjuring, masters of language themselves, one and all, one and all gone on.

You cut a small branch of hardwood and then you fashion a hook by nipping it at a fork. With the hook, you can lift a seething pot by its bail when your spuds and onions get to boiling over, or whenever they're ready to taste. That's the *hookum*. If you know what you're doing, you can lift the lid and judge the readiness by smell. That's the *snuffie*.

Hookum-snuffie. It's believed to derive from Passamaquoddy pidgin, and no, it can't mean anything now. Still I say it. There's something deep in the combination of words, and in many ancient others, that I always loved, and which I still want. That's why I now and then make a hookum-snuffie just to do it. And I never shape one without naming it aloud in the woods or on the shore. It helps me to see some of the last of the genuine woodsmen again, along with their strong wives, and in rare cases even one or both of their parents, all of whom had their special skills. Nineteenth-century figures, really—like me, though of course I'm speaking only of temperament. I'm not one of them, could never have been.

I've come back and back to this corner of Maine for more than sixty years. Its hold on me grows even more powerful in the absence of those great characters I met in young life, more powerful too as, inevitably, the part of me weakens that busts through the puckerbrush for wild game, wades heavy water for trout, or portages more than a few hundred yards at a go.

Every elation here—each bird pointed and flushed, each noble whitetail buck, each loon and moose and northwest wind, with its wild tattered apron of waves and its rushing clouds—is at least equally freighted with its opposite. I ask, in my vanity: how can I surrender all this to others, so few of whom can possibly know the region's history, as I do, by way of its old-time characters?

I ache to see the foxfire glint again in Earl Bonness's eyes, say, as he tends his flame and his smutted cookware. He speaks of driving great evergreen logs out of Mopang Stream. I *heard* him tell about all that. I yearn to hear George MacArthur, who could throw a broad-blade sleeper axe and bury it, time after time, in some not-so-near tree's trunk. He *told* me how and when he learned that trick.

The old ones told me and told me and told me.

George and Earl always claimed they liked to work. Not many nowadays would truly savor their sort of labor, which would kill most modern humans, as it would have me, even when I was twenty. Paid by the back-breaking job, not the hour, and still, like as not, you were hunting or fishing or poaching for food, day or night, in the scant interludes.

The male elders are barrel-chested, deep-voiced figures, who still seem mythic, despite the tempering irony of my older vision. Earl knew what it was to ride the long-logs clear to the ocean, where they'd be gathered into schooners and carried south under great sails to busier ports.

George knew what it was to cut ties through the whole of a winter on White's Island without once seeing the camp in daylight—out by lantern before dawn, back the same way after dark.

George's niece Annie knew what it was to use a canoe for a bedroom.

And I—I know what they told me.

They're all dead now. Everyone else in the world, or so it can seem in irrational moments, lies dead too.

The lumber company blew up Third Lake Dam about forty years back, after moving timber by water was outlawed. Reaching its ghostly site, I heard an eagle scream uplake, but I couldn't find her. I started a fire and waited until the pot-lid danced. I hadn't brought anything to cook but coffee.

Hookum-snuffie, I breathed, imagination transforming those pillars of mist out on the lake to river drivers riding their wood.

2012. The new century isn't all that new anymore, though how recently it seemed so. Now it recedes into one before and one before that and words and phrases call to me: deer *noise on the beach,* are *gone on the clean jump*; a tin cup *wants more coffee*; there are *bad doings on the lake*; a rugged man is *withy*; a big chopped tree is *quite a stick.*

Earl has a habit of slowly filling and tamping his pipe as he starts to spin a story. George makes a certain wave of his hand when he does. *Do you mind the time,* George begins, the verb an old form of *remember. . .*

It's as though I mind Earl scampering over the logs in the boom; soon they'll lift the dam-gates and sluice that mass into the Machias.

George has swamped a spot where he'll drop the first tall cedar of the morning; he spits on his mitts, grabs the bucksaw.

I've long considered myself a wordsmith, and though I do so in my late sixties with a satisfaction that dims as my sense of the literary arts' future does, I don't quite know how else to know things. I go on working at a magic return of what's perished, that old profusion of a beloved idiom, one that lies hidden and hurts me.

Hookum-snuffie. I muttered this morning. *Hookum-snuffie.*

Then I doused my fire, steam wasting itself into the heavens. I said it again, more slowly. It rose out of me on a column of air. I dreamed my old dream: that some word—fossilized, forgotten—could quell an old longing.

George MacArthur with his old sleeper axe.

Photograph by Steve Takach

Cold Time

Weathers and Places

—in memory of Creston MacArthur (1919–76)

Wherever you may be, if you are capable of memory there, can you fetch back that dawn on Freeze-to-Death Island, the sleet jabbing at our faces like some archaic dentist's tool? A small flock of geese drops in among the duck decoys, and without so much as a word between us, we let them paddle around unharmed on the riddled surface. There aren't many geese in this part of the world, and there's something so elegant about these few that we just can't fire.

At length you rise from behind the rock we use for cover and shout, unaccountably, "Off to Cuba, baby ducks!" You pronounce it *Cuber,* like JFK. October of '63. The big birds flush in a tumult of sound, and it soon occurs to us again how damned *raw* it is. As your best friend Earl would say, colder than a frog's mouth.

What elegy can there be?

As a young man, I had a real knack for remembering weather like that, or any. I can still tell you, say, that the winter of '81 brought virtually no snow to the north country. Several April days in '73 were unseasonable, to put it gently; they got hot as a flatiron. My son, your namesake, was not quite two, and I still see the chocolate Easter bunny liquefying in his hand as we stood together in the dooryard. That seems sad now, and did even then, which is curious. The boy wasn't fazed in the least himself.

The candy still tasted sweet; he simply licked the dark streaks from his tiny fist and palm and forearm.

That power of recalling a day or a season's conditions, along with a few other endowments, is about gone. I am quicker to summon the elements from a morning many years back, like that one on Freeze-to-Death, than from a few hours.

But whatever gifts I own or lack, I'll never forget how the afternoon of your funeral shaped up: it was very like that hour of the geese, but this time the nasty conditions, rather than appropriate to a moment of glory, seemed the opposite. The moment marked for me an end to a crucial discipleship, friendship, even son-ship. I watched the chill earth close over all that.

The old saw claims that time heals our wounds, but it's not so much that we're healed as that the wounds become part of us, along with the joys and frustrations and pleasures of any life. They sink deep inside our beings, components now of what people describe as our characters.

In certain moods, the day of that service in '76 seems to have become a perennial one, a present full of sideways sleet and wind. We mourners dodge strips of shingle, tarred paper, and tin, torn by the gale from the Passamaquoddy shacks. Sand and salt blow off the road and sting our eyes as we file into the reservation's small Catholic chapel. The congregation is about a quarter tribal, three quarters white.

It's February, but Big Lake is pocked with open water in the strange winter thaw. Whitecaps show in the gaps, sloshing up and over the ice. Haggard dogs shiver, pressed against the leeward wall of a maintenance shed. I notice a poster flapping from another wall. I can't read it in the blow, but I know what it says: KEEP MAINE'S FORESTS GREEN. It doesn't seem possible they'll ever be that again.

The power has failed clear to the coast.

Though I don't know her, a Native woman limps to my side and tells me she can't for all her many years remember anything like this late-winter weather. She grimaces, sneaking a tea bag under her lip against the pain in a dark tooth, which she keeps touching, as if she had a tic, but it's only that she's unsettled, as we all must be, at least in some measure.

In the brush that borders the parking lot, I see the rusted head of an axe. Fox, vole, and deer tracks meander among the weeds that poke through ugly snow by the path to the church. Two barred owls start yammering at one another, midday dark as dusk. Once you likened that racket of owls to *a good pack of hounds*. Perfect. I remembered, and remember now, the yaps of my last beagle down in a black swamp. Every sensible detail starts a recollection.

All this turmoil—high water and wind and loss of electricity—seems to settle on our group; we mill, uncertain where to go in the dim sanctuary, with its incongruous whiff of incense. Your wife, not you, was the Catholic, and even in death, as in life, you oblige her. The weather, so gloom-ridden and wild at once, settles on Peter Dana Point, this thumb jabbed into the rumbling belly of the lake. I'd like to ask the old Native woman how she knew you, but I don't.

No, I can't imagine suitable elegy for you, for your father Frank, for my own father and brother, for your uncle George, for anyone gone from my brief life. Elegy feels like posture, pretense, artifice.

It would be good to hold something lovelier in mind: your camp, say, on the point. A quiet July night on the lake. This far north—flat country under wide sky—there's still enough light at nine of a mid-summer's evening to look cross-lake. We've strolled east a few hundred yards just to look for what we can, but in the twilight we hear before we see that cow moose and her twin calves wading, all a-clatter, from the Middleground out to Prune Island.

Despite their considerable distance from where we stand, even the younger animals seem monumental, like figures in a procession that could have begun a thousand years ago. It's as if the moose *represent* something, though I couldn't say just what; after all, they're only seeking a place where the mosquitoes are thinner than on the mainland. There's the barely audible luff of a blue heron's wings overhead as it coasts into the marsh behind us. Then a long and wordless hush.

You were eight years younger than my father, and you were both, tragically, about the same age when you died in your late fifties—far, far too young. I'd just turned twenty-three when his coronary killed him, thirty-three when yours killed you. In between, you had taken over in many ways, giving me a sort of graduate education in the things he started for me: woodcraft, hunting, canoeing, pursuits that have ever since constituted the rhythms of my life, even when I'm merely sitting at a desk as now.

Inside the wintry church, I pick out certain crucial visages: dear Earl, who for some reason always called you Gus, as you called him too; Lola, the masterful Passamaquoddy basket-maker, a little your senior; your sweet younger sister Annie. I don't yet know that Earl will live to ninety, and Annie almost that long, that Lola will make it to a hundred or there-abouts. I don't know that my firstborn son, your five-year-old namesake, will have children too, much less that his younger sister will have twins, her baby boy likewise taking the name Creston. I don't know that I and the wife who walks beside me to the pew will walk our separate ways in a short half-decade.

I don't know much of anything.

It's late afternoon now, thirty-five years later, and I lean on my elbows. Out in the shed, I have a couple of ruffed grouse brining, which I mean to smoke for Thanksgiving. There's a good bed of coals in the woodstove beside my desk, though it's not quite genuine cold time yet. Through the study window, I watch a pair of hooded mergansers dip and surface on our pond, dip again and surface. Time may be a perpetuity, I dream, things repeating and repeating themselves. There may be a brighter side after all to that perennial today I imagined a moment ago. The water is cuffed by wind, the minor version of that high-handed blow on Big Lake so long ago.

I could write your name into any of those sentences I've just com-posed, your human nature so enmeshed with nature proper that I still find it hard to segregate the two when I think of you. I glance briefly at a photograph on the desk; it shows you holding up an imaginary shotgun and aiming on an imaginary flight of waterfowl.

The afternoon ebbs, and through the glass door of the stove I watch the fire wane too, its glow taking me back to many an outdoor blaze's end. We sat before those flames, swapping tale after tale, you, at my insist-ence, providing the greater number. It didn't matter whether or not I'd heard a story before; each was new and familiar at once, same as the fires.

In that place of countless waters, the murmur of waves and the lisp of currents furnished insistent under-song to our conversations, and just now the stove's radiant embers and the slaps of wavelets on the pond send me back to a certain early spring.

You and I have just dipped these smelt from one of the local brooks; I can't remember which. We've labored to pull driftwood out of a half-frozen sand spit and kindled it with birch bark, which browned and curled back on itself like some old letter. The heat has galloped across its spectrum. We cook the little fish and eat them right out of the pan when it cools some, fingers for implements, trousers for wipes. Steam rises from our boot leathers.

We finish, and turn attention to a red squirrel and raven as they scrabble over bones and heads we've chucked into the brush. We laugh at this comical skirmish until we nearly weep. Or perhaps it's just the smoke in our eyes, the breeze having shifted. The smoke smells sweet, and the water bears an equally fragrant whiff of tannin, so typical of these red wetland waters. You remark that the bark of the squirrel and the growl of the raven are *rough as a stub fence*. There's a paradoxically honeyed quality to the comment.

I have no choice these years later but to accept, even to affirm, such bittersweet gifts of another weather, late fall this time, the air turned so suddenly clear at dusk that the only haze is inward. It prevails for a moment. Then, through it I discern more fish, native brook trout, curling too. They're that fresh. Another panful. The trout's gorgeous flank-spots slowly fade.

Out on the lake, all done with her own fishing, a loon calls out for wind. Without it she'll have nothing to lift her. Darkness floats down. It's time for all of us, loon included, to make ready for night.

An American poet, to whose work I often resort, in one of his most noted and most misapplied poems, "The Road Not Taken," speaks of "knowing how way leads on to way." I know a lot about that too: once my mind gets started in retrospective mode, this path seems to branch onto that one, that onto another, on and on until only sleep, and at times not even that, stops my rambling. A person's memory can and will go anywhere, everywhere.

Now sunset conspires with the deep orange shimmer of the stove in transporting me to the summer of 1964, when my immediately younger brother and I followed you to Scraggly Lake. It was something of a production to get there in those days, all the way up West Grand, then through Junior by canoe. Not so long after, the timber operations would cut roads to virtually every beautiful place in the territory. Plans are afoot to put four-hundred-foot wind turbines on a ridge above that cherished body of water. But Scraggly was remote territory then.

Once the sun went good and down, at your instruction we took nets and headlights and filled a bucket with frogs from the shores of Jake's

Island. Next morning, we'd hook the little creatures through their lips and toss them out for bass. When our bobbers twitched, we'd throw the bails of our spinning reels and let the fish go until they stopped, then we'd set the hooks.

The bass would be large and stout-hearted. That next night, though, I lay awake for a long time, picturing the poor frogs as they raked their mouths with their front feet, a gesture pitiably human. When slumber did come, I'd dream of an immense frog, wearing a porkpie hat and sunglasses, puffing on a thick cigar. He sat manlike on the aft seat of a square-stern canoe, clutching *me*. I'd wake up just before he ran the hook through my lips.

Your apparent indifference to the frogs' desperate gesture and my revulsion from it, which made me vow right then I'd never use this method again, indicated some pretty basic differences in our cultures after all. You were, especially then, far more a part of nature than I, and nature, as another poet insisted, is red in tooth and claw.

All of this now tells me nothing so much as that some deeper bond made our differences unimportant in the end. I wonder if my brother's turning to vegetarianism shortly after that trip had anything to do with our day of cruel angling. It never occurred to me to ask him when he was alive. I call up yet another line of poetry, terse, poignant, by the late Donald Justice: "So much has fallen." The poem is entitled "Absences."

Way leading on to way, I contemplate yet one more absence, one more late poet, your uncle George, who would be more than one hundred and twenty if he were still with us. No one took greater delight in his performances than you did. You had most of his songs and poems by heart, and I see, just as if you were here with me, the glee in your eyes as you recite this one or that.

In George's era, more even than in yours, the village made its own entertainment. There would be variety shows in a building, gone before my time, out by the ball field. I vividly remember when young people from the village played against young Passamaquoddy on that field. I especially recall the Socabesin brothers, Patrick and Ray, the first a ferocious slugger, the other a dazzling pitcher. The field hasn't been used in almost a generation, at least not for sporting events. The mating woodcock don't whistle up and tumble back to its spring grass anymore. There's an annual craft fair there now, a nice enough event but a different matter altogether.

Back, however, to those old shows. They usually involved musical acts and skits, and as fellow townsmen worked to change sets, George would stand before the curtain and entertain the audience. His pieces of poetry, as he called them, were ordinarily satiric of people, places, and things in town, though at times they could be wonderfully tender.

I once asked George to write down one of my favorites, which lampooned each member of the Boston-based crew that took the better jobs when the new schoolhouse, a WPA project, was built in the '30s. George worked on the assignment at the table in my river camp, gripping the pencil stub like a dirk knife, tongue poking out, eyes squinted.

After twenty minutes or so, he said, "To hell with it!" Writing was something he could do—and almost never did. "Sit down," he almost barked at me. "I'll give it to you." I took the pencil and we finished in fairly short order.

That morning I recognized more clearly than ever how rooted George was in a living *oral* tradition. He composed all those poems and songs in his head, not on paper, and like any made up by his family or neighbors, and there were a lot, they followed variations on one format: a four-stress line, followed by a rhyming one in three stresses.

I'm sure that my poetic inclinations to regular meter and rhyme as means to lodging verse in a hearer's memory must owe something to your Uncle George, as to other fabulous locals. I take no part in the endless and stale debate between proponents of free and formal verse; it's only that I do seem to be all about memory, and always have been, even back when, relatively speaking, my store of it was pretty slight.

You and I sit inside your father Frank's camp on Wabassus Lake, which he and George shared in trapping season as young men, and where your dad lived all but year-round to a ripe old age. George told me how the paper company once demanded a lease payment from the brothers for this property, despite their having used the camp for years and years. Somehow the two found a way not only to dodge the payment but also to procure an actual deed to the land.

I can't remember the details of how they managed that trick, but I do remember the poem he or Frank or both put together in response to the company's demand. At my request, you've recited it for me over and over, until it's something I have by heart too, though I ache to hear your better voice, and George's even better one, recite it. Part of the ballad goes like this:

> *We've hunted on the ridges,*
> *We've trapped along the shores,*
> *And we pray we may continue*
> *Till St. Regis locks the door.*
>
> *St. Regis thinks it owns the land*
> *Where we hunt the ducks and geese.*
> *St. Regis must be gettin' poor:*
> *They want a dollar's lease.*
>
> *We'll see they never get that fee;*
> *We've got things well in hand.*
> *And St. Regis may be told one day*
> *The MacArthurs own the land.*

There's poetry in the very names of the places the older MacArthurs owned in their fashion. Slewgundy Ridge. Jones's Mistake. Dawn Marie Beach. Bear Trap Landing. Pocomoonshine Lake. Porcupine Mountain. Big Musquash Stream. Flipper Creek. Buck Knoll. Slaughter Point.

We were a pair of outdoor companions too, though for far less time, and like those magic elders, we beheld these landmarks in each other's company, and to that extent may have felt we owned the land in a comparable way. I won't pursue this line of reverie, because my thoughts, as they touch on matters that are after all spiritual, will either grow impossibly vague or pretentious—or both.

I look through my study window. Our pond has stilled.

It must be mere coincidence that when we file out after the service, we all notice that the wind across Big Lake has quit dead too, its absence as deep as was its rage. Those places and days blow softly through the churchyard instead, each like a consecration. You have your elegy; the old names deliver it rightly. You knew what they meant; you touched them all—boot, paddle, and pole.

I realize more strongly than ever how lucky I was to know them too. With you. At least a little. It is not enough, but it is far, far better than nothing, the fact that I must settle just now for repeating the names of your ancestors' haunts, which we saw in all weathers, as we did the ones I've mentioned sharing with you. Freeze-to-Death Island. Prune Island. Scraggly Lake. Jake's Island.

It would take a lifetime to include them all; in fact it has.

Creston MacArthur, my chief and beloved mentor in everything having to do with woods and waters.

Daybook, February

I looked this morning at one of my older journal entries. Should I be concerned or impatient that I more and more indulge in retrospection? Even if so, there's nothing to be done; I'm helpless.

The entry, recorded on February 18, 1971, reports that I climbed the small, pointed hill that faced the decrepit yellow house in which my first wife and I then lived with our infant son. I remember that hill as a sort of children's book illustration, a simple, symmetric triangle.

"A hard job to get across Trout Brook," I wrote, "the stream virtually all open even in February, or else covered by treacherous drum ice. What I value now has a lot more to do than it once did with pleasures of the hearth, but there are moments like today when my deepest wish would be to have some natural landmark—hill, mountain, brook, whatever—named for me on a map. The place would prove difficult enough to reach that it would never be 'improved,' say, by some housebuilder intent on The View. No one would go there save those who, like me, wanted just to be there, with no thought of putting the surroundings to some fancied use."

Today I smirk a little at the man, not yet thirty, who rhapsodizes, however tersely and in fact untruthfully, on having settled for domesticity, and I wince a bit at his longing for a landmark in his name. Of course I'm a bit nostalgic for that young man's capacity to feel such vainglorious longing, the one who imagined immortality, even of such a minor sort, within his reach.

That writer was surely motivated, to defend him in a modest way, by his reverence for the old woodsmen and -women, in whose names there were indeed places, however obscure, on maps or at least in local parlance.

The man I am now prays for the places themselves, names be damned—at least insofar as his own is concerned.

That Little Boy You're Holding

Dear Dad,

In a span from 1979 to 1980, I composed a cycle of poems in your honor, which would show up in my second book. I don't know whether I'm dismayed or not that you never had a chance to read it. At the time, I thought it comprised my best writing ever, that it made me look at last like a grownup. Today the whole thing seems sprawling, amateurish, negligible, except, precisely, for its dwelling on your memory.

Whatever their quality, all those poems mention hunting, for which you kindled my lifelong passion. That ardor has stood up against the rants of People for the Ethical Treatment of Animals and the milder disapproval of milder folks, mostly because you showed me that a hunt has a lot less to do with game bag counts than with human involvement in a huge and wondrous process. Non-human too: all those breathtaking dogs! all that splendid game!

From you I somehow learned that hunting is sacramental, that Meaning with a capital M is its real prey—not that you ever resorted to such highfalutin' words about the matter the way I can.

One of the few poems in that sequence I'll stand by is the opening one:

Late February. Orion turned
the corner into the long

sleep, blindness
on the earth's black side,
as you did.
Sleet. Cloud.
Woodsmoke creeping
like a whipped dog flat
to the ground, and heaven
was all occultation.
So the few last bitter lights,
down to Betelgeuse,
in familiar constellation—
they slipped away
before I'd caught the art
of seeing, harder art
of naming. Early
fall now, now again
the wanderers—the winter
planets, memory, restless birds—
begin to shift. It will be greater
darkness if the language skulks, unrisen.
Flesh of my flesh,
you pause to take
quick breath
against the quick descent of evening.
I feel that exhalation
along the throat, I wear you
as I wear your threaded
hunter's coat, my father.
From which in this gust
into night there climbs
—like word or star—
a single feather. . . .

I composed that more than a decade after your February death, and felt happiest with the single feather. To me it suggested that I could offer accurate testimony by talking about the scantest of your leavings, which meant your influence remained lively in the least detail that bound us. My life need not be winter unending, perpetual dark, as it so often felt after you died. I could take such a tiny detail and move from it to the bright constellations. I could see a whole universe.

That notion seems a little like wishful presumption now. But maybe I didn't understand back then what my own poem was trying to tell me. Today that feather-figure seems most eloquent of my ineloquence. Or perhaps it's just that, being older, I have a different response to the same experience. At any rate, I'm most drawn now to the half-line that claims "I wear you."

If I peek into my rearview as I drive to a bird cover, say, and in doing so see my face as your face, maybe that's a mere matter of genetics. In terms of practical life, we hardly resemble each other. You were the small businessman, I the "artist." You were steady, deliberate, handy with tools; I was impulsive, moody, and, relative to you at least, mostly thumbs. You were more than fond of that sentimental dog-and-cat story, *The Incredible Journey*; I was and remain a certified book snob. So on.

Still, "I wear you/ as I wear your threaded/ hunter's coat, my father." The notion holds up. I don't of course literally still wear your hunting clothes, though I did for as long as they lasted; but I'm still hunting for meaning, for a shapely world—the same way that you, like me or anyone, must have done for all your too brief life. In other words, I see how wrong I must have been to think of your road as free of the melancholies. Whose road is ever paved with such exclusive good fortune?

I was supposed to be a poet, but however much I loved you, and that was plenty, I stuck on surface details for too long a time, caught up in our visible differences. It's taken me all these decades to see how you and I shared a lot of spiritual garments too. To see that now is not, however, to give you up as Hope's muse, which you've been for many a year. Yes, it turns out that one's history must be revised day by day, maybe minute by minute, but some part of it will remain intact.

How can I make myself clear about this? How tell it plainly?

You'd often ask me, precisely, why I could never just say things straight. Well, forgive me again. What actually motivated this letter was the chance discovery of an ancient photograph of you and me; seeing it, I felt my mind take off. Not straight.

Can you let me follow it? As if I haven't already . . .

I wonder if you're sweating in the picture. Like you, I sweat like a racehorse, even when most around me are shivering. You and I shared a high furnace. Odd that I thought about this when I found the snapshot. The photo's old enough to leave such details to my strange imagination. That's true of so much between us.

I can see the trees are leafless, but that could mean early spring, late fall, or winter. All the deep-southern seasons are warm by our standards. So, yes, you'll soon be mopping your brow; I recall the gesture well.

But you have better reasons to sweat. There you are in Gadsden, Alabama. Some place to be commander of an all-black company of troops! You and your men, unlettered country kids one and all, are waiting for European deployment, hence the uniform you wear; you'd think fright would show up on your face, then, but mine is the one to show it.

What would a kid of eighteen months know about world history in the making? That clearly wasn't what troubled me. No, there's another chain of events, the personal history we share to this day, one that makes our expressions on the Gadsden street seem completely logical. I'm confused there, afraid. You are trying to soothe me.

I don't mean I recognized the half of all this until well after you died at fifty-seven. I obviously hadn't had many recognitions of any kind back there in Alabama, which couldn't be my fault, baby that I was when you were taken overseas.

It wasn't your fault, either, that you also missed some recognitions. You never knew your grandchildren, for example. As much as anything in this world I regret that they can't experience your affection. Happily, you missed the day when a brain aneurysm blew away your second son, who hadn't yet reached thirty-five; nor were you there when one of your daughters was brave enough to affirm her lesbianism. All those unpredictables. How would you have responded to them?

But then does any of us really want to know each last detail about our fathers or mothers or children or dearest friends? It may be partly because you're gone that I can mention a few particulars concerning you and me. Of course, since you'll never really be gone, you can hear me clear my throat here, hear me sigh. I scuff my mental boots in imaginary dirt. As if it were deer or trout, I have to sneak up on what passes for frankness, even though compared to most we were very open with one another. It's just that I've learned how real candor can threaten a wound. To someone. It may not deliver on the threat, yet the threat will lurk.

To wound your memory, however, as I need scarcely say, is the last thing I desire, which is why I'm feeling my way, traveling with care. In this later life, it doesn't take much sometimes to rock the world. A child can't imagine that: he thinks growing up will fix everything.

As the rearview proves, I resemble you physically nowadays, more than the photograph predicts. Why would that rock anyone? The likeness of son to father shouldn't be shocking, and it wouldn't shock in the least if I didn't so often note the resemblance chiefly when I'm sunk in some darker mood.

The set of our jaws, the raccoon rounds under our eyes, the sparse hair and incipient jowliness all give me pause, because—in the years before your coronary, and the forty-plus years since—you've been in all respects the model of promise. You led a short life, but left, so far as I've ever discovered, no enemies. We could all aspire to such an accomplishment. That our faces most resemble each other's when I'm feeling other than hopeful menaces me with incoherence. What if my sustaining vision of you is in some measure concocted, if naïveté has blinded me all my life? Is the truck's rearview more accurate than my own? Must I completely recompose our common experience?

This damned snapshot kicks up a lot of rabbits, so many that I want to chase them all. Or none. Every memory or thought seems random and relevant. I can touch the past anywhere, and you're in it somehow. Even when you're not.

There's a day at nursery school, for instance, which I'm sure you never knew about; you were still off somewhere killing bad guys. Since early September, I've been competing with a certain rival to rule the playground, especially its wooden playhouse, into which a yellow jacket has just flown. Or so my classmates believe. I'm apparently the only one who saw it flare away at the last minute. Not even the rival will go inside.

How, having entered that green box and come out again, can I convince anyone I've pounded the little hornet into the dirt? Don't my playmates demand to see the meager corpse, at least some remnants of it?

Unchallenged, my charade makes me king of the mountain for a long time, right into grammar school, my classmates all taken in.

Yet I can't be fooled by my own monkeyshines. I'm frightened all the time. Of what? I usually can't say, the fear non-specific, though I do recall one particular scare from the same general period, this one after you've come home from war. "A grasshopper bit me," I tell you. It must be August. The air above the Swamp Creek meadow is almost liquid; the meadow itself is eccentrically mowed, the 'hoppers hiding in the hay stubble; that old, pigeon-toed Farmall tractor seems to doze at the edge of the woods.

These things I do know, but I can't be specific about other matters. Grasshoppers don't really bite, of course, at least not painfully; and yet—this is one of the things I can be sure of—there's some early pain lying under this memory. Tears widen the circle of perspiration on your chest once you gather me up. That circle represents succor at its purest to the child in your arms. Or no: the very impurity of it succors him, the non-ideal somehow implying the ideal, as he'll one day learn was true for Plato.

There is earth and effort in that odor, and although I could never have told you as much, there's some encoded notion of honorable adult maleness, a notion that guides me today. All that rank, brawny, bodily presence suggests the sort of armor in which I'd like to sheathe the vulnerable: battered women, gays, the racially oppressed, and above all my children and their children. I could still use it too now and then.

It isn't that you'll protect me from all the truly harrowing stuff—death, time, disease, injustice—which I'm too young anyhow to recognize; no, it's just that for my private, inscrutable miseries there exists a literal solvent. Mansweat.

It sometimes feels nowadays that nothing can be solved. Not with you vanished, along with one or two crucial surrogates who too briefly survived you. Or that's the sort of thing I mumble whenever I see my face looking like yours in the rearview. I know I melodramatize; it's a cursed habit, damned near a hobby, and finally inexcusable. But in such moments I do crave some warm refuge from the challenges faced by any adult, particularly those awful night thoughts of mistakes and omissions, of people whom I may have hurt.

I must even have hurt you, made you feel inadequate. Kids can do that, I've learned. In fact, there's already something in the photograph that causes me to re-experience my own genuine moments of inadequacy in forty-some years of fatherhood. Though it may be my usual inclination to guilt, it looks to me in the snapshot that you are there in a way I may now and then not have been for son or daughter. You'll be leaving Gadsden within the month, right out of the country; meanwhile, you try to comfort that little boy you're holding.

I can't find any pictures from that time immediately after your return from the European theater, but my mind retains one indelible image: I see a stranger in khaki, paused in our driveway, a cone of evening light falling on him from a gap in the clouds, as if to emphasize his grandeur.

Then the picture comes alive: Mom sweeps me up and rushes to greet this Captain Lea. As you take me from her, I scream my lungs out. I have, after all, been the only male in a house full of women—aunts, older girl cousins, the wives and children of men at war. I've been king of that mountain too, and you're an intruder. The way you clutch at my mother is a horror. I won't take it!

Did I occasionally resist you in some similar way as I grew into young manhood? No doubt. It's a thing sons do, I suppose.

You probably never read John Keats, since, besides that dog-and-cat tale, you didn't read much, least of all poems. I only think of Keats because he once objected to calling the world a "Vale of Tears." He called it, rather, "a Vale of Soul-Making." You vanished too soon from that vale, but my guess is that, pressed for such definition, you'd have said something akin in your own words. Which makes you still a model, as I say, an inspiration.

Maybe at last I've learned from you that to be a father, a more crucial calling than writer's or hunter's or teacher's or fisherman's, isn't a matter of being king of any hill, of having it made. Instead, although the most strenuous phases of my parenthood are, somewhat to my sorrow, behind me, fatherhood should be a matter of effort, which one rarely lets up on. I think that's what I keep seeing in my rearview mirror, through my unKeatsian tears. Like you, I'm struggling to make a soul worth passing on for my children to wear. It takes a whole life to do that. I think those children may be more consistent and thoughtful in their own parental efforts, but perhaps they learned a little from my example after all, as I from yours.

Sometimes the struggle has felt almost physical, as if I were with you, following a hard-going bird dog through heavy brush, the way I did when I was just slightly *more* than a little boy.

And as I say so I get the smell of mansweat—the solvent, the small salvation.

Love forever,

Your Oldest Son

In my father's arms prior to his tour in the European Theater, Gadsden, Alabama, 1942

Daybook, March

Yesterday, it was winter when I climbed the ridge just west of my writing cabin; today I climbed into spring!

Spring, with its tobacco-and-mushroom odor in the leaf mould; spring, when, out of idle curiosity, I nicked a red maple with my knife and watched it gush. Leaning close to the base of the tree, I watched the infinitesimal snowfleas swim through old granules.

On the way back down I lay a few moments on the south slope, patches of which the season's strong sun had thawed and dried, looking through squinted eyes at the absolute sky. I permitted myself some magical thinking: *If I will it to be there, a bird may cross that blue blank.* There appeared a bird. I thought it was a crow at first, but it looked too wide in the wing and soon became a high hawk. How languid its coastings.

When I stood and took a few steps through the blueberry bushes, I almost stumbled on the spine of a winter-killed deer, its ribs likewise pointed skyward. I thought how the hungry dualisms grind us all.

So I got to my feet again and kept heading east, toward home. Just before an old boundary wall, my pointer froze on a very early woodcock. I walked over and flushed it. Its whistle seemed spring itself, quicksilver.

Beside our largest vernal pool, the red-winged blackbirds would soon come back to chant from the cattails. I noticed a shimmer along one bank: the pseudo-sunshine of last fall's withered ferns.

I reached the gravel road to our house, its ditches tuneful with runoff.

My chain of observations somehow led me to my forty-year-old son's elementary school days, when, with what seems in retrospect the same surge of energy as mine just now, he'd run from the car out onto the playground, where he and his mates delighted in the suddenly usable swings and seesaws.

Overhead, he-ravens rasped, swooping and quarreling with one another over she-ravens perched a few hundred yards into the woods.

Skunks had begun to roam again, as I saw on one of those glistening mornings. One bedraggled animal had been clipped by a car out near the town pond, where the children would swim come summer. The poor thing stood mid-road, blood in its mouth, swaying its head back and forth, as though it searched to see what had happened, and how so quickly.

I wanted not to fix on that image from long ago—feeling too fit, too good and glad—so I didn't.

Spring

Dirt and Blossom

I piece this narrative together from some things the late Bill White told me, and these were sketchy, as he conceded, even to him.

At the very turn of the twentieth century, Bill said, there were two savvy woodsmen. I think their names really were Harry and Charles; in any case I'll call them that. They had a lean-to camp in the Musquash country, smack in the middle of nowhere at all back then, and vacant of humans, because it was almost entirely marshland.

One thing Bill heard from Harry and Charles has stuck with me more vividly than any other. It had to do with a dead man. Neither of those older woodsmen could reckon how he came to die. No blood on his body, no other mark of violence. He looked clean and pure as an altar boy.

It was never found out just who he was, or so Bill insisted. I'd bet the authorities—such as they may have been in that barely populated region and in that era—did learn a name, but I never challenged the claim, nor so much as asked any of the other veteran citizens about the story itself, let alone about this detail, and I can't ask them now. I never speculated, because the victim's identity was not and is not the point. Indeed, his lack of it seems more important.

It happened that Harry and Charles were hunting on a certain day, and no matter it was May. *This was early times,* Bill pointed out. *If it wouldn't've been for fish in the water and critters on the ground, I imagine folks would've starved.* No, as a rule the old ones didn't wait for some season to arrive; they shot and jigged and netted all year round.

That morning, a thunderstorm raced in from nowhere, the downpour something ferocious. Harry and Charles took for a thicket of cabbage pine, which clumped in an old burntland that another lightning storm had fashioned long before, eliminating what few larger standing trees there may have been. Boughs grew dense enough in that tangle to keep the men fairly dry. They scooched inside to wait on the weather.

Then one of them looked out and noticed the corpse.

No, not a corpse, but only the bottom of one bare foot, which glowed with each bolt from the sky. The two hunters knew of course there had to be a body too; they just couldn't see it. Whenever it fell, it must have dropped right over the near bank of the stream, that bone-white sole the one thing left to show. The men might easily have missed it if they'd sheltered elsewhere. They told Bill they wished they had.

The two hunters didn't speak for a while, but each of them knew what the other must be thinking. Neither liked the idea of what they'd find by that little stream but when time arrived they'd by God *have* to go find it. You couldn't just walk away, although both admitted to Bill that they might have done so if there hadn't been the two of them. *They was each other's conscience,* Bill said.

In any case, they stayed under those scruffy pines long after the storm moved on. Whoever he was, after all, would be in no hurry now himself. The men left him resting right there until they could puzzle out what on earth to do about him.

What those old poachers did do at length—well, for whatever reason, in Bill's retelling that was a bit of a blur. No doubt they contrived to paddle him out at length. But what he more clearly remembered was their coming out of the shelter when it faired, and suddenly noticing a twisty but thick-trunked small tree: a pear, of all things.

Now so far as anyone ever knew, this godforsaken spot had not been a settlement, not even for tribal people; there wasn't enough solid or level ground. There were no white man's cellar holes either, no remnant fire pits. Nothing for miles but marsh and wind, with here and there a horseback of land to tread on. The fruit tree, just into tiny leafage, was the only indication that the place might have been lived in after all. And how had the pear tree survived the fire that had swept this solitary patch of solid ground?

How, further, unless a seed had been carried by a bird or an animal (from where?), and unless it had been dropped just here, was a pear standing on its spot at all? The only answer seemed that someone, in some dim time, had made a dwelling. Could there have been a dooryard, could this tree have been one of many that amounted to an orchard? If so, why *pears*? Bill also wondered how they'd identify a tree so rare in those parts anyhow. He wouldn't have been able himself.

It was barely true spring, the pear's petals just fallen. A few ribbons of ice held out along the water's edge where it ran under alder shade. The corpse lay in that darkness. That fringe of ice chilled the hunters' souls, they said.

The story still chills mine, though that's to describe its impression too simply.

The hard gully-washer from which they'd sought refuge in the green-growth had splattered mud on the dead man, but sodden pear flowers too, which at first they took for old snow. The poor fellow lay naked otherwise, no sign of clothes anywhere they looked.

And the dirt-and-blossom trousers, the mask and cap, as one of the woodsmen told Bill, *They wouldn't make no difference to him now.*

Bill White, who taught me the art of handling gun dogs and who told me this yarn.

Photograph by Steve Takach

Daybook, Mid–April

I set out a while ago up an abrupt hill, a favorite of mine. Now a muted glow in the air makes my climb worth the effort.

At the modest summit, a raven, old familiar, scolds and swoops, protecting the nest she keeps each year in the very same slope-side pine. I'm frustrated: I wish I could simply tell her I'm harmless as always. I'm not even looking up at her anyhow, but down to where the spated river sluices past its banks, whose grasses are slower to green, it seems, than usual.

Two yearling deer stand, pastern-deep, on flooded ground that will soon be broken and planted. Come fall, shivering cornrows will wait out there for the thresher.

But I guess I'd have to admit to the hen raven that some moments back I did in fact look up. I'd settled down on the earth, face skyward, feeling in my bones that the life I led still had a fair share of future in it.

The turkey vultures didn't think so. There never used to be vultures this far north. Everything is change. Climate. Custom. Demography.

Three of the vultures glided low; I could stare right into their eyes. I'd been dreaming how wide the world was, even this small portion I hid in and claimed for my own, so I stood up to scare them off, along with the thoughts such creatures can bring, disconcerting and banal at once.

But now I keep watching the edgy deer. They feed and startle, feed and startle, trotting a few quick yards, all splashes, then pausing again to look over their shoulders. They can't know where I am or who, up here in this all-subsuming shine, staring down at them, their hides silvered as the sun is silvered by the river's mist. Silvered like the galvanized domes of silos on the Gales' failed farm. Silvered like that commonwealth of blackbirds, which gleam from the farm's heartbreak hedge of tall dead elms.

Now Look

What follows, I confess right off, is far more tale than report, however firmly I may have founded it on things Mattie told me. It doesn't mean to speak ill of her husband, a beloved mentor of mine, after all, who told me many a story of his own. But I loved Mattie too, even if in her later years we stopped talking the way we once did. I hope she didn't think of me as a contributor to John's decline, though I suspect she did—as perhaps, unwittingly, I was. I know less, not more, about such matters as I move along in life.

How accurate can it be, then, my vision and version of her on the day I remember? I imagine her scowling at my back through the bedroom window, right up to the point where I cross the Tannery Bridge and disappear on the other side of the river alders. Having found her man asleep in his stalled truck, I've just rolled him onto a ratty cot in his shop. I'm headed back to my camp for my last day here of the summer. I'll be driving home when the sun comes up tomorrow.

It's getting on daylight, and Mattie can see that the back lot's maples already have a touch of flame. Winter's around the corner. She has testified more than once to how she loves this time of year, or used to, that little hint of color, and the wind coming soon to streak the northward lake with foam-lines. The salmon moved into the shallows in late September, and she'd stand on the bridge as a girl, dropping pebbles into the river, just to watch the fish shoot out into quicker water, then sidle back under the cutbanks.

That wind has stiffened up just now. I watch a pair of ravens fight it to get upriver, gaining two yards and giving back one, flopping around like laundry on a line. Mattie's mountain ash berries aren't even red yet, but the cedar waxwings were still mobbing them as I walked out of her dooryard. How she adores the *light* off those birds! She's told me so.

"You don't have to live with that old man," Mattie growls at where I just stood. Or something like it, I'd bet.

But enough of this contrivance, this present tense. Years have gone by since that dawn.

John had been a hero of mine, but also of Mattie's in a much different way, back when they were courting, when weather meant a different thing or two. As soon as the deer came into rut, the town was all women in daylight. She missed her husband then. She missed him a lot of the year. He was the best-looking of the bunch, no two ways about it. He'd get done in the woods on Saturday evenings, and the two of them would go somewhere: maybe only a walk, or sometimes a canoe ride, or even a dance if there was one.

It didn't matter, dancing or walking or paddling, he was always turned out nice. How on earth could some bachelor get his shirt that white? You saw it, plain and crisp, even after dark. Same with his teeth. He had them all in those days, and they'd almost blind her in sunlight, even if he did chew like so many of those hardhead lumberjacks. *Handsome enough to make a mare eat her own bedding.* I remember her using that expression, as if she couldn't help it, then blushing ever so slightly.

But it wasn't all how John looked, she insisted. He could just do things. He drove logs in April, first one hired, best paid but Biscuit the cook, who'd been doing the drive since John was a baby. That river scared Mattie half to death until he quit, too old for it, he said, at forty.

In winter, when he cut railroad sleepers, he was top hand as well. The woods boss would go bunk to bunk every evening, taking tally. "Fourteen ties," someone would say, and that would be pretty consistent, give or take one or two, right down the line. But it'd be twenty-two for John, or twenty-four, even thirty-two once, after someone tipped him off that a younger fellow named Billy Gibbon meant to beat him on at least a single day. John just worked himself almost off his feet for a week or so, a proud man. Billy couldn't stay with him, went right back to the pack after that spell.

And every one of those sleepers was an A. You got a quarter for an A, fifteen cents for a B. Of course this didn't seem like money now, Mattie admitted, but that was then. There wasn't enough decent cedar for this sort of chopping anymore, and Lord knows what people used for railroad ties; seemed there was scarcely a train left in the country. But in those days plenty of good trees stood right below town, so John could be home nights, not like during the spring river drive.

He went away on that drive the very first year they were married, which was when she really learned what lonesome meant. She couldn't sleep for the thought of him treading around among those logs. How could he claim to love such a business? Making ties, he left early, but she could get up with him, she'd wait for him all day, and at least his Sundays were free. There was plenty to do while she waited, of course, especially after their first child Sammy came, but tending the baby or keeping house or chunking up the furnace or splitting kindling—no matter what, she'd be thinking of evening.

Now look. I heard Mattie say that a hundred times if I heard it once.

As I hiked down to camp on the early morning I recall, I imagined her, all slept out, a lot bearing down, especially the one memory—or three. The children, each of them dead before twenty. But that's another story. There was John out in the shop again, not even knowing he was in this world. He wouldn't know until eight o'clock, or even later.

Mattie had taken to wearing a pair of wool trousers. His. He was skinny by then, and she gone a bit to girth, though she didn't care about that a particle. She put on an old shirt, his too, not white. Then she made herself trot downstairs. The way to keep going, her mother always said, was to keep going, and she knew what she spoke of: Ma shingled her own roof as an old woman, and it never leaked a glassful, even though she moved out that same year.

Old? Sixty-five is all her mother was when she did that roof job. She had a little income from the Navy people, after Mattie's father got himself killed in the first war, and it just barely paid her way down to Florida. Mattie told her not to go, but she did. Stubborn, forever stubborn.

Mattie argued with her. You need something besides sunshine every last day of the year, she said. Fair weather and nothing else, except maybe one of those hurricanes, and they could kill you dead as a smelt—none of that can be healthy, Mattie told her. But Ma went along anyhow, never listened to a word.

Mattie wanted to be like her in some ways, but she also wanted to live a quarter-century longer anyhow. Seventy-nine now, so she guessed she was on her way, because her mother had only been seventy-five when she passed.

Mattie always meant to have Ma's drive but live to a round hundred.

Come to think, though, why would she want that now? There was a time she pitied her poor mother, all those years without a man. Did the pity still make sense?

Any way you sliced it, if John woke up sober enough to speak, even he would tell you a fellow could play checkers on his wife's shirttails. Well, that's me, Mattie always said. She couldn't change if she wanted. Or maybe she was changed already; she didn't like to think so.

Now I see her standing in the kitchen, doing nothing, only studying the electric teakettle, that drooling bastard. There was a crack in the spout: you'd lose a cup for each you boiled. She meant to find herself a new one, because John wouldn't get around to fixing things, not the way he acted lately. He wouldn't even drink coffee anymore, too busy drinking another cup.

The electric kettle sat next to the range top.

Electric kettle.

Range top.

All kinds of things changed, some for the better.

It was still nice to fire up their old wood-burner cook stove now and again in fall or early spring. Take a little chill off, save on oil. Not for old times' sake, though. Old times? Try making cedar chips on the kindling floor first thing if you forgot the day before or you were just too beat to do it then. She told me they called it *killing floor* down south. She couldn't remember who taught her that, but it was a better name, especially if she had the morning sickness, the way she always did so bad with both boys and especially with little Emily, God love her.

You'd get the stove het up with the cedar, then slide in a few sticks of whatever hardwood lay to hand. She was always quick about it, same as she was with anything, but it was still half an hour before the kitchen felt near comfortable.

Washer-dryer.

Water heater.

Lord in heaven.

Maybe she hooked up the kettle and found a teabag and a bottle of molasses. That was her habit. They'd claim there was nothing in it, she said, but she always felt better for the molasses, and others could think what they thought. Pregnant or not, she never put much else inside her in the morning.

John lay out there in his bedroll, or maybe just in his clothes, on top of that stinking cot she'd burn up if she had a chance. Mattie was proud to say she hadn't been inside the shop two dozen times since they moved out of it into the big house, and that had been a long, long stretch. She could barely lay her eyes even on the outside of the shack, no matter she'd been the one to build it. That was in their first married year.

Sometimes, she swore, she could still feel the cold of that fall; a drop in the thermometer would bring the feeling on. Weather came early and rough, a foot of snow by Thanksgiving, and her in the dooryard bare-knuckled, putting in studs and joists and stringers, fitting the little windows that old man Patcher gave them for their wedding. They needed a real place to live now, not some canvas tent, summer all gone. John did as much on the place as he could, but he was in the woods more than he was out, so yes, a lot of the job fell to her.

She nailed on the waney-board siding, the only kind of lumber they could afford. She mightn't have looked at the shop so meanly if John would prise those ratty wanes off and put up some clapboard, or just some butted planks. She was damned if *she* ought to be the one to do it; she'd done her share, and some. But he was always too busy in the old days. And now look.

It could be she wiggled her fingers that morning, just to thaw the memory. She'd always do that when she spoke of those days. She even confessed to me how one morning, while she was building, she felt something strange down below, and came to find out her backside was held together by her own frozen sweat. She had to dip her hands in a water pail before she could tend to herself. I could see the minute she told me she was sorry she'd shared a thing that personal with a man not even kin. Good old days? she scoffed. Don't ask *her* about that!

It was nicer to look out the other side from the shop anyhow, past Addy Benson's house to the sidehill, which had seen a lot of changes since the burn, Lord, thirty-six years back. After the fire, the popple took over for fair there. Those trees looked white as birch in winter, then lovely yellow on top in spring, then all the leaves riffling in summer whenever a breeze blew. *Money trees*, some called them, not because the wood was good for anything beside excelsior but because when those leaves went down in October they looked like coins on the ground. The hill was all stunt pine now, hardhack in the clear spots. A popple didn't live long; most of them grew, fell, and rotted in what seemed to her like a few recent months now, not years.

That blasted shop could rot too, and Mattie wouldn't care. It made a start for them once, but good riddance after they got the real house up. There were a lot of better days in the new place, which they still called it. The territory got known for bass in the lakes, and when they paved the road into the village, John actually made a dollar or two off the sportsmen. He took them to cast for smallmouth and he looked after their summer places. The sports were the real money trees. You just put up with some of them, but there were a decent few, she allowed.

I hope she included me, hope at least she knew I meant well. She may have wondered why I couldn't save John, but I just couldn't, not for all the money trees on earth. No one could. That's just not the way these things work. I wish it were.

John did all right with the guiding, and every little inch he stood off from a falling or especially a floating log was a good inch, far as Mattie was concerned. And it wasn't just the danger: when he only worked as a guide, they could spend more time together, as a married couple ought.

Those good years lasted a long while, but they didn't last forever. What in creation did?

Did the teapot spit on the oilcloth? I know it never whistled a note, and Mattie complained on that, said it was a nuisance. She was the one to have burned the hole in it, though, so she said she shouldn't complain. One day she put it on the stove, same as you would a regular.

Did she yank the plug and fill that cup with the two cub bears on the outside of it? The bears were looking down from a pine for the first few years she owned it, but the tree part wore off, and the bears seemed to be flying. Angel bears, she called them, not trying to be funny.

Under the cubs was a wad of gray stuff that John used to patch a seep, because she wouldn't give this cup up for her life. Getting it fixed, even rough as this, was one of the few things she just forced him to do, because their Sammy had made it when he was about eight. He worked it from a jar of clay she bought him. There weren't going to be any more Sammys. No more cups. No more floating bears.

Sammy and Herbert were born in the new house, but she rode clean to Calais to have her daughter, who just wouldn't come out on her own. That was in an A-model Ford, older than God, but it had been the only rig around anyone believed would last the trip. Mr. Patcher kept it nice. John started crying as if *he* was the baby, leaning in from the rumble seat so she almost went deaf with the roar of him. As if she didn't have plenty to put up with anyhow—more than thirty-six hours' worth before she so much as got into that Ford.

Old man Patcher had gone away in his younger days and made some money in a trucking business. He was a fine old fellow, she had to say. Drove his car right along that night, never a word, determined. Thirty-three miles of frost heaves and ruts, and Mattie's bottom about falling out.

Then came the chloroform that smelled like death even days after. They dropped the cloth over her nose, and it wasn't a minute until she saw a bunch of lumberjacks rise right up in the air, but not a one with a face she could recognize.

I heard about this dream many times; it had a hold on her, and why not? It does on me. The woodsmen floated toward the sky, and then all of a sudden their clothes fell off. They were nothing but skeletons underneath, the bones all blue, and down on earth was her dead mother, shouting about it all from the far side of the river, calling Mattie to her.

It didn't make any sense. Only a dream. Her mother was home and well when Em was born. She wouldn't die for quite a time. Yes, Florida killed her, Mattie swore. Nobody went away in the winter. Not in those days anyhow. Some did now, but they never lasted if they stayed down there. It wouldn't be long before their kids were getting themselves to Florida on a bus to drive their parents' car back north, hauling the ashes to the town graveyard.

Oh yes, that was some trip to the birthing room. If she ended up in hell, Mattie told me, she'd be ready for it after the labor and the ride in the old car and the feeling when she woke up with a gash in her so big you'd think a pole axe made it. They cut her daughter out of her, is what. Yes, she'd be ready for hell, even if what she already had in late years was not your bed of roses like they raved about in songs.

I was a grown man that morning, but a young one, and I just didn't know from Toby's ass, as he might have said, what to do with John these days. And I couldn't think of a way to cheer Mattie up either.

John had drunk all his life. There weren't many loggers who didn't, only those with sugar, and even some of them were pretty quick to pull a cork. They liked their tea, as Mattie put it, and more than liked it in quite a few cases. There wasn't too much you could do about the matter if they got that way. She'd learned that much. And she learned a woman looked out for herself, because nobody else meant to do it for her.

She'd say this for John: he never harmed her, never so much as slapped her, and not just because he knew she wouldn't be one to take things exactly like a lady. The hardest part, as she said to me early on— and I knew what she meant, odd as some might find it—was that John quit telling stories once the liquor took over. It surprised even her to miss them, because she'd already heard every last river tale known to man, especially his.

The one about Eddie Stamford and that same old man Patcher was among her favorites, and mine too, though you really couldn't call it a lot more than a one-line joke.

Eddie and his family lived at the top of the only real hill in the village, up where the fire tower still stands. The tower went out of use quite a while back, only a place for kids to climb to the cabin, just to say they did it, maybe to smoke a cigarette or drink a beer someone bought them.

Eddie made the river drive for many a year too, and his wife Bess didn't feel any more kindly about it than Mattie did. John always said he was a good hand on the trip, but the minute he got home he'd take to drinking again. There went most of the river money. Once upon a time, John judged him for that. What would he say now, Eddie long gone, his liver bigger than a backhouse seat? John wouldn't have much room to look down on him.

Eddie was doing some work for the town, repairing the wharf on the lake. As John told it, he somehow drove a six-penny nail right through his boot and through the meat, clear to the wharf's planking. He had to be pretty full if he could manage that, you'd imagine.

This was in the Depression, and Mr. Patcher still the only man with a car that could be counted on to run—not the same one as when he rode Mattie and John so they could cut the little girl out of her, but a good one too. Now Mr. Patcher was a fine man, but he had a little of the Devil in him too. After Eddie made his way to the old fella's place, all the way up that same awful hill, there was blood just sloshing out the hole in his boot. He knocked on the door and pointed down when it opened up.

"Look here, Ben Patcher," he said, "I run a spike through my toe out to the wharf. You got to take me downriver for a doctor or I'll get the lockjaw sure as hell."

The old man stared Eddie dead in the eye. "Look here, Eddie Stamford," he said. "You get back to the job. I'll put a chair to watch you, and the minute your jaw starts to set, I'll run you right in."

Just as I say, no better a story than a lot of others: it was really *how* John told this one, or the next and next, that tickled Mattie, me, or anybody who heard it. He had Eddie and Ben Patcher right pat; if you closed your eyes, you'd imagine each one of them right there.

But you never wanted to close your eyes, because it wasn't just a voice John could imitate; he noticed little details, like how Ben squinted one eye when that Devil was in him, or Eddie gave a little hitch at his belt with his wrists about every third sentence, as though his drawers would slip off if he didn't.

And John got even more inspired when there was an animal in the story. He had a gift of looking like any critter he named. If he spoke of his childhood bull terrier, you saw that dog, all nerve and shiver. He'd do an eagle staring down on a lake, a treed bobcat, a swimming deer, anything. John just knew how to live inside what he described—hard to explain.

No, he never laid a finger on Mattie, never so much as shouted at her, not even when she figured he almost had a right to. Her tongue flapped like a raven's as a young woman, and she'd admit it. There was even a time or two when she hauled off and laced *him*. He only stood and took it.

When the drink got hold of him in his seventies, which seemed like overnight, he didn't get cross, just quiet, run out of things to say.

Sometimes he scarcely talked at all for days and days, fussing around in that damned shop, or bouncing along some old skid road at five miles an hour, or moping around the cemetery till he passed dead away. He'd freeze out there one night if he kept at it.

I went on telling myself my own tales about Mattie, trying to gain some sense of what she was going through. I hated this whole drunken business with John, but not as much as she did. I'd idolized the man, but no, I wasn't married to him.

It hurt me to think of Mattie as merely putting in time, killing off hours, because that had never been like her, any more than John seemed like the old John these days. Lately, if they did go visiting or out in the canoe or just to see some fish hawk or eagle nest or raspberry tangle or the sun going down on one of the lakes, he was like a ghost. She might as well be on her own, she claimed. It seemed as if he'd found some girlfriend and couldn't quit thinking about her.

That other woman never used him right, but she stayed on his mind. No, not *she*: Just a damned jug.

Time went by like a short night's sleep. Here it was 1933, and Mattie, all out of breath, telling her mother: "I'm over to marry John" and running out of the house like a hen on a journey. Her mother didn't like that. Always a funny duck, or why else would she wander off to a place full of snakes and alligators? But Mattie was eighteen, so Ma couldn't do much but watch her bang out the door and wobble across the bridge on her boughten high heels.

And then here it was sixty years later, and all that business no more than a memory. Here she sat, drinking electric tea out of a half-broke cup.

Mattie and John are gone, along with so many of their generation—all, in fact. But I still imagine her in her chair that morning, in what turned out to be John's last year and her next-to-last. She may suddenly have tasted something salty and found, to her astonishment, that she was weeping. Maybe she called herself foolish, right out loud in her kitchen.

But how am I to know, even if I think I do? Say I have some nerve to make that claim, and I won't contradict you; I guess I do have nerve, but I can't help it. You tell yourself things, and you hope they make sense. What else can you do?

Maybe she peeked out the shop-side window and saw him, or what was left of him, hair all anyhow on his head, blinking like an owl.

That was a man who hewed thirty-two A railroad sleepers in one day. His shirt shone white as his teeth. He wrapped her up in his hard arms all night long, even in a nasty, leaky old tent.

Now look, I hear her say.

The Turkey Cure

$\mathbf{B}$y middle spring, nearly every time I walked down our road with my pointers, we flushed the broad-winged hawk that nests in the same tall pine each spring. She's been a genie of renewal, and the life force in me surges to study her tail as she flies, the severity of its black and white bands somehow standing for the distinction between seasons. Dark winter. Bright spring.

This year, thanks to last autumn's bountiful mast, the chipmunk and red squirrel populations had apparently grown threefold, a great thing for a hawk, of course, and for all the other predators—fox, coyote, fisher, and so on—whose energies have thrilled me from boyhood.

And yet this time around, such tokens of rebirth and others, the loosing of freshets, budding of shad and thorn apple and chokecherry, ruckus of peepers, chatter of kingfishers, all failed to inspire me. My tendency to construct fancy poetic resonances in nature, however irresistible, struck me as more than ever inaccurate, in fact as absurd. The very idea of finding allegory in a hawk's tail like that, for the love of God!

Surely it was the suicide, not even a year old, that had me down all through the winter. This beautiful boy, my oldest son's bosom friend, had fallen into a contemporary trap called crack, and ended up with a homemade noose around his neck out in California.

But if this horror had proved a motive for my long despondency, I might have chosen from others: the obscene death by cancer, say, of my father-in-law, who got too weak at the last even to cough for himself. A bright, handsome, volatile man, he'd stuck to being a journalism professor, loathing the job for the final decade, waiting out retirement, at which he was diagnosed all but instantly. No time for his writing aspirations, none for the book-length project on that Cape Breton copper mine, on its place in the history, sociology, mythology of the region, which he'd never get to visit after all. His idea died when he did.

Or I could batten onto my mother's life-threatening aortal operation, from which she did recover, but which forecast the closing of a crucial cycle: she who'd borne me would leave me. Years before the surgery, I'd had an odd vision. Standing on the stoop of my Maine river camp, I looked upward and imagined the heavens' vault closing itself like a womb after birth, killing any dream of reversion to that snug lair, which all through life a child will crave, however unconsciously, when comfort seems otherwise impossible.

Closed out. The world blank as a sheet of paper, as the sheet unmarked by my wife's father, in which blank realm my role would be methodically to evaluate students' papers, mostly poems and fictions, not to write any more of these myself, not to write anything at all. Rather, I'd continue to take my turns fetching and carrying our kids but would be no proper father, down in the mouth all day and night, nor a proper husband to my excellent wife, who deserved worship, probably, but at the least some friendship.

My agenda? Cook my share of so-so meals. Do my share of dishes. Watch the years mount, the yellow leaves of spring becoming the yellows of autumn overnight; the hare going white from brown in a blink; warbler ceding to snowbird; my body slumping. My fifties would be my sixties would be my seventies. Tomorrow.

Attending all this was a changed regard for hunting, which, however inexplicably to some, had had so much to do with my self-regard all life long. I'd considered myself, particularly, one of the better grouse men around, but by virtue of a chainsaw accident that radically cut my leg and my woods time in the preceding fall and a rock-bottom bird population in the past few years, the tasty little monuments to success lay sparse in our freezer. It was also hard to make a young dog under these circumstances, and a made dog has forever been a far more important sort of monument.

I began in fact to surmise that my skills in this crucial portion of my existence were dying, like too many men and women around me. If there'd been a time when I seemed a person, as one of the great Aldo Leopold's students once marveled about him, to whom the game just seemed to come, that time looked to be fled.

The first morning of Vermont's turkey season, I had a time of it just to coax myself out of bed in the pitch dark. Uncharacteristically, I sensed failure before the fact, anticipated my fatigue, which would set in by noon and put me behind in my journeyman jobs. I'd have felt contempt for such tiredness, of course, in my naive youth, when a duck blind at dawn segued into six hours afield behind a pointer and then into an evening's carousal until the small hours.

I did have to acknowledge that the hardwoods looked beautiful at the top of the first ridge, their leaves pastel, their every story melodious with migrants. The abandoned twitch roads were so thickly clotted with bluets that they seemed still to be snow-covered. Frogs croaked in the spring pools. Wakerobin showed in wet gullies.

A lovesick barred owl called not far off. No tom turkey answered that sound, however, or my own imitation of it. For a month, there'd been turkey sign all over the four ridges I meant to roam that opening morning: I'd seen a gobbling jake in our very dooryard; I'd heard other toms uphill from the west bank of our pond. But on this day, no response. None, that is, save that owl's. Defying its reputation for wisdom, the bird coasted silently, inches over my head, and perched a spell in a gall-sick butternut. Moments passed. The bird went on disenchanted. And so, given the late drift of my spirits, it was too easy to construct crude allegory: the world had ceased answering me, or answered now in unsuitable ways.

I trudged home well before the law said I had to.

Work, appointments, and travel conspired to keep me off those highlands for almost ten days. I felt a bizarre gratitude for these obstacles, because I could moan with self-pity over being deprived, but with no obligation to take up the thing I was deprived of. For someone as mixed up as I, that meant the best of two bad worlds.

And yet at length I did feel an old obligation, or a trace of it anyhow. I would mount the hills again after all. It seems my better self had retained some flicker of longstanding hope, in however obscure a guise. And that self had its reasons: on reaching the granite table that caps the first ridge, I was immediately greeted with a gobble.

The call must have blotted out my melancholies. Or at least I don't remember them from the ensuing hour or so. I do recall surveying the terrain, simultaneously judging with my ventriloquizing, gun-ruined ears the location of the tom. I would need to drop to his elevation if I hoped to call him in.

Well, I knew the country if anyone did. I turned directly away from the gobble, which now came with a heartening frequency, doglegged to a woods road that ran under a knoll to the west, and then crept back, the knoll covering me until the road petered out by the red oak stand in which I guessed my turkey strutted.

The guess proved pretty accurate: he was moving among those woods, just on the other side of a horseback, some two hundred yards from where I quickly set up, my back to a lichen-swathed slab, my right foot pointed in his direction, Browning on my cocked left knee, veil drawn over my face.

For a start I tried no more than a soft whimper and chirp. It was early, the sky just pearling. The turkey yammered right back at me, or so I believed, and I whiffed that ozone scent that I needn't describe to any hunter of wary game; my heart beat in a shirt-stretching cadence, and— despite the chill of a north-country dawn—tiny drops formed on my cheekbones. I slightly lessened the crook of my left leg, to see if it would hold more steadily in a different position. It did.

Everything felt right. And yet, rather than coming my way, the tom started working south, climbing up one more elevation. I was patient. I didn't over-call or hasten to relocate. Minutes crept by, the bird's voice fading by degrees, before I took stock of the land again. At last I stood, then circled back to the east, because I knew another hill-hidden trail, the beat of deer and hare, that would provide quiet and easy travel and would put me at the bird's level again, about parallel, I believed, to where he now sang.

Again and again I established myself at what appeared optimal places. Again and again I heard the gobble go dim and dimmer, always to the south. In fact and in honesty, then, there *were* moments when my mopery did return. Everything, I told myself, seemed auspicious about this hunt, except that I didn't have the requisite skills anymore to end it as I wanted.

Still I rallied from these instants of despair. I had enough experience to realize that if the problem lay only in my calling, this tom, spooked, would long since have quit his gobbling. He must already be with a hen, I figured, and perhaps more than one. If I were to get a look at him, it would not be by way of deception but of ambush. Unable to turn him, I'd need to head him off.

Most of the ridges on our property run north and south, but one is perpendicular to these. Turkeys often describe a circle in their morning rambles, so it occurred to me that this tom and his coterie might well come to that odd ridge out, turning east along it to regain the highest ridge of all, the one where they'd probably roosted. If that bet proved right, he'd eventually be traveling an almost knife-thin granite strip some hundred yards above the pond, a good lie for me.

The locations of the tom's cries suddenly seemed to be shifting more quickly, which meant I had to get up there in a hurry. I trotted to the edge of the ridge, then all but skied down, so abundant were the oak nuts on that flank despite the foraging of the winter deer herd, the spring rodents, and the turkeys themselves. Now and then I felt brief burnings above my left kneecap: adhesions popping under the ugly scar from my Labor Day accident. But this discomfort left me unalarmed: my mind set on being where I needed to be, I even believed that the tearing of those adhesions would do me nothing but good, would turn me loose.

And in fact, hitting the bottomland, I broke into a run, feeling less awkward and leaden than I had in months. A single hooded merganser, sojourning on his way to Labrador or wherever, made to flush as I hurried by the pond, then simply dipped underwater, waiting for me to pass. I might see the little clown again on that pond, a notion that filled me with curious delight.

Even with a quick glance back, I noticed that the mist over the water had abruptly become general, the world now soft-edged everywhere, the top of the scarp I'd just tumbled down completely vanished. The damp combined with the sweat of my exertion to fog my glasses, which would have to be clear by the time my tom came into view, please God. I yanked them off and held them in my hand like a relay baton as I raced onward.

My breath came with surprising ease. "Not bad for an old guy," I whispered to myself, feeling my cheek muscles tighten in a grin. Well behind me, I heard the pointer bitch let out a hound-like howl from her kennel, nothing in it to alarm a gobbler. Indeed, I thought I heard the turkey answer her, and persuaded myself that the answer came from exactly the right quarter, not far from where I meant soon to be.

I envisioned the bird as I ran: He'd be coming out of a certain hop hornbeam grove just now, stepping into the higher hemlocks, his snood turgid and scarlet, his tail clenching and unfurling, his hens fossicking behind him.

And before long, he'd reach that strip of stone.

The fog was everywhere now, showing itself in weird little pilasters, each like a man walking quietly overland in a company of his familiars—thin, benign ghosts.

You'll imagine me single-minded, as I imagined myself. But truth is, I found much to notice. By the pond's standpipe, I'd seen shoots that in a month would bend with the weight of wild iris; above, daylight's first vulture, which hadn't been there and now suddenly was, languidly riding the updrafts; a few stubborn gray frogs still quacking at each other, bank to bank; a woods-smell like chamois.

My boots left prints in the bluets. Again I thought of snow as I watched the earth pass under me. At last, hearing the turkey startle the air in that hemlock grove, I started to climb. As I did, the delusion of infinite stamina began to undo itself. My breaths turned to something closer to sobs. Yet I went on, hiking now, to be sure, not running. So much depended on the next few minutes.

The tom could not have been more than a few hundred yards away when I reached height of land. Squinting, I discovered a bathtub-sized depression, as if placed there by Providence, in my granite slab. I sprawled in it, belly down. There was even a cleft in the rock, like the archer's slit in a medieval turret, through which I could see 90 degrees or better, and through which, fate allowing, I'd be able to shoot.

The turkey remained as persistent in his call as he'd been since I first heard him, and, no doubt about it, he was headed my way. I slipped my eyeglasses back on, pulled down the veil, then cursed mutely as the lenses clouded over. I could see next to nothing.

I reached up under the veil with my gloved right hand, rubbing a small circle on either lens. Within seconds the circles misted again. The bird's gobble was as loud by now as my frantic thoughts. I pushed the glasses to the tip of my nose and peered over them, but things appeared at least as blurry that way. The cruelty of my circumstance seemed incredible, or so in my exaggeration I figured.

And then a cold breeze kicked up. Some may think this all sounds too scripted. I can't prove a thing, having been the lone human in that place. I do know, though, that such a wind arrived. I can all but feel it again right now. My vision went clear.

And the gobbler quit calling.

Long, long minutes yawned. I imagined the tom, with those eyes that beggar comparison, had somehow seen through the rock to where I hid, fussing with my misted glasses. Surely he'd scooted off with his harem, not to reappear.

I have said before and will again that I've had more moments of bounty in my life than I deserve, ones that—who knows why?—I haven't had to deserve. That foggy morning well behind me now, I think back on a bright and dear boy's terrible self-destruction, and how badly I responded on hearing of it; I scarcely recalled, say, that my wife had loved that young man as much as I ever did; it was dully that I observed the innocence of my smaller children, the decency of my older, and in particular the bereavement of the oldest son, whose friend more than anyone's the victim had been; I failed even to acknowledge the very splendors of the earth and air and water among which I'd long dwelled, or the blessing of my fine physical fortune, which I'd taken too often for granted. Today the depression I felt throughout the months leading up to that hunt seems to have been so easy, even lazy.

A tall bird walked forth, stirring the fog with his bulk, silent. Behind him trailed an abundant procession of hens. I saw the flock through that cleft in granite. My gun barrel rested on a rocky spur, parallel to the pungent, pine-needled ground. The tom had grown cautious, as a tom will uncannily do in such moments, yet he continued to pick his way toward me, lifting and gingerly replacing each foot like a heron, until at last he stood exactly where I wanted him, his beard thrust forward like a bowsprit, glinting with dew. He stretched his neck, cocking his head northward. I squeezed the trigger.

I thumbed back the safety and hopped up. As I rushed toward the spot, I found myself expecting no sign of a bird, expecting to awaken, that is, from a dream whose emptiness would leave me cursing and whining on that shoulder of stone. But there the turkey did lie, in all his splendid gigantism. An impossibility, but there indeed he lay. I set the shotgun on the earth, leaned over, grasping a horny shin in either hand.

At my touch the gobbler appeared to come back to life. He kicked one leg free, his great wings pistons, his whole frame pumping to reach the cliff face just ahead, down which he would surely hurl himself, never to be found. I held tight, my heels digging vainly for purchase in the wet granite, the bird manic in my grasp, like some unruly dog on a leash who has spotted a squirrel, or some weirdly autonomous machine.

I didn't think so then, but now that desperate wrestle seems a comic chapter in all this. What must I have looked like, a man of two hundred pounds and more being drawn by the will of a wild thing, a dead one at that, toward so freakish a conclusion?

But the man prevailed.

The recognitions that came to me that morning are hard to explain to a non-hunter, let alone an anti-hunter. Perhaps I'm less a hunter than once I was, but on that spangled ledge it struck me that I not only possessed at least a few remaining skills but also, and much more importantly, that I was simply blessed by circumstance.

I remembered it was Mother's Day, and conjured the winsome smile of my spouse. I reckoned how nine months earlier, I'd sawn my left quadricep to the bone—and gotten off with three days in a hospital bed, four weeks on crutches, a spectacular and storied cicatrice the only residue of the whole ordeal. Meanwhile, a logger I knew on the west side of Champlain had cut his femoral artery, which I just missed doing, and died before he could be gotten out of the woods. Yes, my fiftyish body was slumping some, but it was certainly a lot sounder than it might have been.

And subsuming all these emblems of my rare welfare was what I can only call a spiritual insight. I will abuse it, as I have done before, as any pilgrim must, but there it was. My mother, like Breck the suicide, like Amico the cancer victim, must die one day. As must I. As must every last one of us. And yet for a moment, a truth shone clear: be receptive and you will receive. Not that I had truly willed my own receptivity; as I say, it seemed to have been bestowed.

I felt, I feel, a great gratitude to a certain wild turkey. The anti-hunter winces. Be that as it may, walking down the steep ridge, the gleaming bird slung over my shoulder in all its heft, I recalled, as I do now, the perfection of the tom's coming to me. I had put myself in the right way, or something had, and a wild creature obliged me. What had been random was, for a spell at least, coherent.

Daybook, May

What I observe from Big Musquash Stream could be the set-up for some witless, formulaic joke: *This kingbird chases this eagle . . .*

Anyone who knows about an eagle knows he's a bully who robs ospreys and other predators, furred or feathered, of their water catches. Glorious as he may appear, he also runs crows, ravens, and vultures off road-kill and other upland carrion and quarry.

He's our national symbol. Make what you will of that. I'm not out here for complexity, or even complication. I'm taking a break from all the clutter I can. I want things as simple as simple knows. Still, I've suspended my morning paddle here beneath the *whoosh-whoosh-whoosh* of the mighty eagle's wings to watch the kingbird—no more than a flycatcher, after all, no matter his magisterial name—as he jabs at his adversary, and reflection has begun. Once that happens, it's hard to drown it merely by wanting to.

I'm all but sure we're too early in spring for chicks in these parts. The eagle must have been looking to pillage a clutch of eggs. Or maybe he was after the sparse flesh of the incubating hen herself. Or both the meat and eggs.

There being no one to debate with, I silently ask the air, with idiot grandiloquence, *Who, knowing the wild world's unfairness, still believes in harmonious nature, let alone benign design?*

I'm addicted to the natural world, but certainly not because it ratifies the cozy oneness of the universe, nature a realm of profligacy and waste in so many regards. For every hatchling that fledges and flies, for instance, how many do not? Five? Ten? A ghastly percentage for sure. The fearsome creatures prowl the wide earth, hour upon hour, daytime and nighttime, in pursuit of the fearful.

But again I try to avoid thorny issues, to satisfy myself here by praising what looks like plain and reckless courage. Though in spite of myself, I know I'm imposing human values and qualities on what I witness, as I watch the smaller bird in its dartings I imagine emulating him, forgetting my weakness and flying right into the face of whatever oppressor I know or have heard of. I can't be alone in wishing, single-handedly, to right every wrong, remediate every injustice, humiliate every bully. I want all this even though in my soul I know murder, rapine, and dispossession will go on carrying the day, and the day after.

As the eagle will.

This kingbird chases this eagle. No joke at all, I realize, envisioning the downward spiral of fluff and feather, rent from the poor she-kingbird's breast, the gold of yolk smeared over the savaged, intricate nest.

But what's this? I'm deceived just now into thinking that foolish valor may pass for advantage after all. The eagle is finally chased over Amazon Mountain, sinking behind the tree line's green hysteria, its legion May-time shapes and shades. And the dauntless little kingbird flits back to its mate.

But he's farther upstream from me now than he was before this insistent springtime current, scarcely perceptible from shore, made me drift all unaware back down the river.

Ownership

—in memoriam, John Engels (1931–2007)

I'm in Anchorage, Alaska, when I get the cell phone call from my pregnant daughter-in-law, who is nothing if not an angel, in this case an angel of sorrow. I've been standing here and browsing Philip Roth's *Everyman*, which apparently chronicles a lustful codger's last seasons. The tale may be rough going for a sixty-something like me, even one who happily looks forward to his first grandchild this coming autumn, but I mean to buy it anyhow. Owning such a book will feel a little like courage, as if I could simply stare its relentlessness down.

To hear the bad news in a bookstore, even one too cutely named "The Title Wave," seems apt. My friend of more than thirty years, the poet John Engels, is about to be dead. I knew he was headed for back surgery while we were up here. I knew he had heart problems. But, blithe as ever, I didn't figure he'd suffer a series of coronaries under anesthesia, that he'd now be in coma, and would soon be taken off life support.

John will be gone before we get back to Vermont.

It's also apt that together with my second son, who's living and working here, I will be looking for rainbow trout in the Kenai River tomorrow. John was an avid trout angler and the best amateur designer and maker of flies I've known in six decades of fishing. He turned out gem after gem, each as deft as his poems, which are a grand part of what I'll remember him by.

My wife and three of our children are considering other reading prospects on other shelves. I go to the counter, buy the Roth, then step outside to bawl.

I'm weeping for John, of course, whom I hoped the Vermont cultural movers and shakers would at last and rightfully designate our next state poet. That can't happen now. Nor will the two of us ever talk again face-to-face. Nor will I read new work by his hand, but must dwell on what remains, some of the best and most scandalously under-noticed work of its generation.

Nor will he and I wade another trout river together, though in fact, owing to his arthritis, we haven't in fact done that for some years, and of course, sore joints and age aside, the trout fisheries we once cherished have woefully degenerated in his lifetime and mine.

Lifetime. The abstraction has suddenly turned particular in John's case. I can demarcate it now. It's an integer.

It's unnecessary to add that my sorrow comes too because, at 64, I realize that John's 76 is a lot closer down the road from me than I've let myself think. I'm truthfully not sure I remember particular events from when John was more or less my age now. I do know that my oldest son, the expectant father, was in his mid-twenties back then, and our youngest child, that leggy near-woman of fifteen in there by the Young Adult section—hell, I thought nothing of loading that three-year-old into a carry pack and heading up one of the local hills.

I'd done that with all her older siblings, and just now I call to mind a certain hour in January or February of one of those years. The afternoons had come back out of darkness, and a feathery snow brightened the end of day. The son whom we visit here, now the size of an NFL lineman, lay asleep in the pack.

There seems nothing demonstrably special about the instant: a thumbnail moon above, the clouds behind me between orange and gray, the little brook I step across to head toward home tuneful under its ice. I'd witnessed many similar moments before, and I re-witness them in memory all the time, as these pages have made plain. But just then, feeling the warmth of the child slumped against my back, I had one of those precious moments when the universe seems as skillfully engineered as it could ever be.

Standing here in such reverie, on 4th Avenue in June in Anchorage, Alaska, I can't say why this reminiscence possesses me. To describe the quality of that earlier experience, I'd try a word like serenity, but, like any abstraction, that would cartoon the feeling. Perhaps I encountered what Paul described in a letter to the Romans: the presence in which *we move and live and have our being.* Why wouldn't such a thing transpire at a height of land?

Of course, the mountain I've remembered here on the street, or any of the nearby Whites and Greens in upper New England, would scarcely earn the name in this state. Not that my local eminence, Mt. Moosilauke, isn't as high as any I can see from this urban vantage; it's just that each of these Alaskan mountains is so young, rising almost wall-like right up from the ocean, where sea lions and sea otters and orcas cavort, where halibut of two hundred pounds flap along the floor, where king salmon the size of sharks migrate up the rivers.

Everything is simply more monumental here than at home, where our sugarloaf mountains testify to eons of wear, seeming to slump toward the incredible sea, not so far—especially by Alaskan standards—to their east. This year, a young cow moose wintered over at our Vermont home place, but next to the moose in this region she would look like some odd dwarf of the species. There is bull kelp as long as a school bus on these strands. Even Alaska's mosquitoes make our own appear small. Tomorrow, though I don't know it yet, I'll take a rainbow trout on the fly. A nineteen-inch trout in our own waters is a very nice fish; the one in my net will be that many inches around.

I will not roar with pleasure over that fish, as I would have in my twenties. And yet for all that, I've been pleased by my abiding capacity for wonder on this trip. It may be somewhat reduced from what it once was, but it's still very alive. I'm looking forward to the float, to contemplating a glacier, to all manner of things, especially in this beloved company.

But I have left the company indoors. Outside, I remember another signature moment, just after the oldest son was born, when I walked out under late December's round moon, and climbed through two meadows to a stone fence just at the edge of a stand of white birch. I sat on a rock and thought about things, chiefly the miracle of a child, everyone asleep in the small yellow house downhill. I had, and still must have, the woods-rambler's yen, or perhaps anyone's, to be alone when considering the big issues, whether sad or joyous.

Things are a lot less than joyous just across the road on a patch of green. Though rough laughter now and then rings from it, the sound's somehow assaultive and resigned at once. Some of the winos and addicts—most of them, sadly, native people, farther from their spiritual homes than I from my literal—lie unconscious on the new-mown grass, whose bracing odor seems out of kilter with all I see of humanity there. Others pass their Sneaky Pete and weed from bench to bench.

I am living a miracle just now, and one miracle a day ought to do me, even if, perversely, I can sometimes forget that.

I'm no nuisance to passersby myself, not likely even much of a distraction. I'm not noisily choking on my grief. No wailing, not so much as a sniffle. Instead the tears seep, turning my T-shirt to a chill bib as an ocean breeze washes me. I squint into the sun, which will be here more or less all day and night. What time, in fact, is it now? Noon, though it could be 10:30, a.m. or p.m.

But even if I make no spectacle, I can't somehow stop, can't seem to pull myself together, as my late mother would have put it. This was a woman who actually boasted about showing no tears either at her husband's funeral or her second-born son's. Sad to say, liquor likely had something to do with her state of mind, too.

There's a bar near The Title Wave, too busy for the time of day. I used to know that kind of place. Its clients stumble in and out. One of them, a young man though hard-worn, reels toward me with his spiel all set. When he sees me crying, though, he simply mutters *God bless you*, a remark for which, however routinely offered, I feel deep gratitude.

I watch him make his way along 4th, taking up most of the sidewalk as he goes. Decent-Honest-Citizens retreat into entryways. Not that I blame them. The man got close enough to me I could smell the barroom —smoke, urine, liquor, and sweat—on his grimy overalls.

The bar, I calculate, sits on the next rung up from the verdant hell across the street. It would be easy enough to turn my present emotions merely maudlin, or to quash them altogether. I could wander inside.

It's been some years, praise be, since I've considered such an option. There aren't any bars near where I live, to be sure, and one doesn't want to be known as the fellow who buys twenty beers a day from the local general store. So what one can do is drive to the hideous chain-store pharmacy several towns away for a two-liter bottle of Listerine, which has more alcohol in it anyhow than the equivalent of beer. One can deceive himself that the antiseptic smell will fool everyone, not least the cops, who—speaking of miracles—have never figured into his life.

Jacked up on mouthwash, I drove the dirt roads of northern Vermont and New Hampshire for hours, listening to corny country singers lament the loss of their livers and hopes, making myself feel bluesy. The encroachment of tasteless McMansions on the hills I used to hunt, the road-salt rust on the bordering evergreens whenever I hit tarmac, the twang of steel guitars and the hiccuppy vocals: I could turn all of these into a bleak eloquence. Of something. But the emotions weren't mine; something tellingly called spirits owned them.

Now *I* want ownership. I'll own the pain of John Engels's passing, along with the other sadnesses that course through my brain on this Alaskan block—bar and bookstore and tick-tack souvenir shops at my back, permanent sun in the sky, human ruins lurching in and out of doors around me, or slumping on pavement, or sprawling like piled cabbages on that lawn cross-lots.

I'm not the only one who ever felt these melancholies. I know that today. In fact, whatever other cockamamie convictions I've held, even drunk I never considered writers any more "sensitive" than the next man or woman, except perhaps to language, and maybe not even that: I've known half-literate woodsmen-raconteurs who'd put most of us to shame. Yet I'm the only one who has access to my particular versions of sorrow, and that suddenly strikes me not only as important but also a sort of consolation. I shall never surrender the metaphorical deeds to such property.

I could be lying on that green patch over there or elsewhere, and only a Ph.D. education and attendant rhetorical talents—call it bullshit; I won't stop you—ever kept me from doing so. Those, and the grace of a countervailing spirit whom I choose to call God, unaware of a better word.

Although I don't stop my weeping, laughter suddenly pierces it. I remember a moment in Dewey Hall at the University of Vermont. Our mutual writer-friend David Huddle had invited to campus the director of an MFA program, in which John—then with most of his five kids in college—aspired to teach part-time. The woman was to read her poems, and John to express admiration of the work, to win the visitor over.

David had held a barbecue prior to the reading. Perhaps John overate or had one beer more than was wise. It got stuffy in that hall, and the poems from the lectern were dreadful. Intended to be racy, they were just gross; calculated to put us bourgeois on edge, they proved so tedious that John nodded off beside me. Except for jostling him now and again when we sensed a snore in the making, my wife and I let him be, his sleep adequately resembling rapt, closed-eye concentration.

Enter the famous June bug.

It had made its way through a high window in the rotunda, and, in the manner of its species, was bumbling clumsily about, batting at the ceiling, rattling off the chandeliers, a brief diversion for the stupefied listeners. At the moment of the thing's appearance, however, my wife Robin and I both knew it meant trouble.

After a few more tedious recitations, everyone having more or less forgotten it, the June bug dropped with a loud *thwack* onto John's bald head. He lurched upright, spilling his bottle of water, bellowing something like *HOO-AH!*

He was not offered a contract.

The incident still makes me chuckle even here on 4th Avenue. My mind is going wherever it wants, the world both funny and tragic, exalting and bitter. I think for no reason of the cliff swallows' holes in the high banks of the Connecticut River, from which I flush hundreds of the birds as I pass in my paddles. How does each remember which hole is which? How do we humans know where we belong?

Then I think of my children and wife inside the shop, as well as the two older children, who have not come on this trip. The firstborn son crafts custom electric guitars back in Burlington, John's home city. The instruments are works of art, and I'm as proud of them as their maker must be, though I'm even prouder of his character.

I think of that grandchild developing in his good wife's womb. I think of his immediately younger sister, doing God's work in Brooklyn with immigrant and ghetto kids, not accompanying us just now because she is placing fourteen hundred of them in summer apprenticeships.

Too bad it has taken me all these six decades and more *truly* to understand what unconditional love is, but I'll own that too, with all my own apparently sound heart.

Lines from John Engels's late poem "Angina" occur to me as I make for the The Title Wave again; I'll look them up soon to be sure I have them right:

After awhile, everything calms itself, and I can stand
and walk away. And beginning right now
down will come the suns one after another.
What sends me this comfort? What
is this brightness, precisely not the light of glory,
by which I consider the garden, and it stares coldly back?

Rest peacefully, friend. No one put things any better than you could, though in this case I disagree with one particular: just here, just now, the light of endless sun in Alaska does seem, precisely, the light of glory. Yours.

I'll own that too. I'll take it home with me, against a garden's cold stare, or anything's, anyone's.

John Engels, dear friend and nonpareil poet of the trout stream.

Daybook, June

The trophies, I recall, skulked in the deeper pools. But as a boy, I only needed current, a high-floating, over-dressed fly, and the splashing abandon of smaller fish. The light stayed and stayed.

Hendricksons made a cloud above the riffles; nighthawks—such as we too rarely see now—sliced through that cloud with a *boom,* audible despite the river-yammer; even songbirds darted out to pick off the duns; the brook trout, green as spring's grass, sipped at the film.

Though I have grown past boyhood and then some, coming long since to prefer the warier browns and the slacker water, that quick run of home stream will remain the only notion of paradise I need to know. It was, after all, more than fish that brightened those upper reaches. The same sentry beaver crossed every evening below the rips, towing, it seemed, the same blond aspen whip. Low mergansers flashed around an open bend and gone, like a thought I didn't quite have time to shape.

And the water itself seemed to possess all the cleansing power ascribed to it by the first baptizer, who cried in the wilderness. To think of that water in later life would lift my mood in classroom, office, kitchen, bed.

Only a boy could truly love such fishing. Brush crowded the banks in much of the stretch so that it seemed half my flies broke off behind or before me, air swarming so densely with black flies that I'd bleed before I could tie on others, and fish so puny I'd sometimes skip them across the surface on setting the hook. But these very drawbacks left that part of the river to that boy alone.

That boy, I know, is continuous with what I now call *I,* but something about him also seems quite different.

The *I* that I now am does visit his old haunt, but must do so entirely in mind. Even so, much comes back: the smell of sun on stone there, spray on hands and forearms, late light leaking through the broadleafs, trout, nighthawk—all still jewels.

And they still renew and cleanse, those headwaters in mind, the stream's mild voice speaking, I sometimes believe, of ancient mystery, like words of some divinity, specific meanings cryptic but crucial.

Appetite

—for Annie Fitch (1920–2010)

Right after your daughter called to say you were gone, it occurred to me—hardly for the first time—that some platitudes survive by being true. The one that leapt to mind was *Time flies.*

You were almost thirty years younger than I am today when we came into each other's lives. I was a kid, not yet twenty. Now I'd travel north to your tiny Maine village for the funeral, nostalgia traveling with me, as it seems to do more and more in my later years. This time, at least, the mood would have its justification.

I stood with my wife and siblings in the town's two-acre graveyard. So many lay there now, including members of your parents' generation, men and women I'd also been privileged to know. Late May, but the hardwood leaves had yet to grow a full inch. Downriver, I could hear an angry raven protecting her nest from some interloper, real or fancied. A kingfisher chattered her way toward the river. There was that wet, fecund smell in the breeze, the sun peering out now, then hiding, reappearing, hiding.

I looked for a rainbow, but no.

The world was going on, impossible though it seemed.

Someone—who?—would eventually move into your rambling house on Tough End. There were those—my daughters, I'd bet—who knew at least the ingredients, but maybe even some of the magic, that went into those irresistible pies of yours. Someone would watch the sun rise over your camp on Lower Oxbrook Lake. Still, things were altered forever.

When word first reached me, I spoke my cliché out loud. And when I looked back on my own life in the many years we knew one another, I wondered: What can I show for this time that has flown? A bag of modestly successful literary work. Eleven collections of poetry, a novel, a book of nonfiction and one of criticism, this last irrelevant.

But in fact it all seemed irrelevant just then. Or at least none of my compositions had been so involved in my supposed learning as what I'd gotten from you. I plain can't imagine how my existence would have looked without you and your many neighbors over generations, while I easily imagine it minus my Ph.D. and books. That tells me something.

Yet how might I give even a précis of all your teachings, which, unlike so many of the world's moral arbiters, you practiced far more vitally than you ever preached? Preachment wasn't your medium. I can't provide an iota of what needs saying here; I'm a man of words at a loss for words.

As another cliché puts it, *You had to know her.* True. And to know you was to know, far less by way of commentary than of example, what counted:

> Treasure your friends and family.
> Be honest.
> Don't deal as you've been dealt unless the deal has been good.
> Don't speak ill of others, no matter what they've done.
> Value every day of your life as, and however, it unfolds.

In light of that last tenet, I remembered an earlier crisis, one of several you were not supposed to survive. That had been half a decade before, when you were eighty-five. The same daughter, Ginny, called to report she'd taken you to the hospital. Again.

You'd already lived ten years past the heart attack that doctors said would drop you dead the night it struck, or at best within mere months. You kept defying the predictions, I'd bet, precisely because you considered every day after an even greater gift than ones preceding, and this despite the sad loss of your husband Bill, the diminishment of your stunning physical strength, the bodily aches of any octogenarian.

I remember talking to you after a checkup, at which some cardiologist, noting a severe lessening of heart function, suggested an operation—not, however, without warning that the procedure might induce another attack, a stroke, paralysis, even death.

"How long you give me without it?" you asked.

"Two years at most."

"Wonderful," you told him. "If they're as good as all the ones since that first spell, I can't complain."

You lived another eight years.

I will always think of you as one with an appetite for life. Such triteness keeps occurring to me, but I know exactly what I signify when I apply it.

On the night I recall, that appetite, for the first time ever, was slack. You were the color of a bruise, your hair a shock of white bramble, your eyes flaming with fever from within their dark hollows. I thought you resembled certain grotesque literary creatures I'd considered in an age gone by, back when I was cranking out that obscure screed, my Yale doctoral dissertation, "Gothic to Fantastic."

Of all the things to come to mind! That old mess of words means less to me than words can say. But why on earth should my thoughts have leapt back to those wretched days at the end of graduate school in the first place? Why picture a younger self struggling with his mammoth chore, his impoverished pen suspended in air? Perhaps it was your appearance and its likeness to a dimly recalled illustration—workshop of Doré, I believe—for some well forgotten tale about a damsel, whose chances of salvation seemed dim as yours in that metal bed. You looked like the monster, though, not the damsel.

But again, how could wild fictions and pictures matter? Why piece all that ancient rot together? The moment demanded better. I held your hand, rubbed your back, taking turns with my good brother Jake, and wondered, How can I or anyone fit together the notions of *Annie* and *Dead*? Nothing like that made sense: you were, after all, as much a force of nature as water or wind. You devoured the world, both natural and human, chewed on it, though gently, and spat it back at us in handsomer guise.

Once, while still-hunting a trail down to Wabassus Lake, I ran into you, a large doe slung over your shoulders, blood freckling your mackinaw. In that moment, and many another to follow, I believed you were some raw-boned goddess who embodied the abstraction *Strength*. It rose from you like your frosty breath. Later in the month, when the venison had aged, I took a meal from that deer with you and Bill. The meat was good. My God, it was good.

Though I sought to hide it, I knew despair in your hospital room. To counter the mood, I tried to batten onto moments like that one in the woods or at your table or others equally joyous. That older, academic past proved a stubborn bully, however; I could not will it away, any more than in those days at Yale I could will myself into an open north, however much I longed to. That was the north—idyllic and hardscrabble at once—of which you were and remain the exemplar, the queen.

At night, down that dismal New Haven street, dismal I'd go for my jug of gin, seeking to flood away my paper's rank inconsequence, and my own. Then came sodden bouts of sleep, of dream-attacks by the very monsters the paper was meant to make sense of and couldn't.

After some years, I fell on significantly harder emotional times than the Yale ones, however bad I'd imagined those. I landed, a bit oddly for me, in a series of rather New Age group therapy sessions. The leader always began with "guided meditation." He instructed us one day to imagine walking through woods, stepping over a brook, and turning into a cave. He said we'd find someone inside who embodied courage and endurance, and must ask that person to be with us in periods of torment. I needn't tell you whom I saw inside, her face lit by an open fire, as I'd so often seen it before.

I should have known. You'd been with me all along. I know you've been with me ever since, even after your permanent physical departure, but even more crucially than before my visit to your fire-lit grotto.

Whatever these weird associations as I watched you shift and shiver, I thought I might live with how you looked; you couldn't have been a monster if you labored at it. What I couldn't accept was your pain, manifestly clawing its way over every inch of your skin, into every pore, along every sinew of your valiant old frame. That misery had to be awful, because you complained of it. I'd never heard you grumble about a thing, so that was proof enough for me: This, to summon further cliché, was it.

My brother and I drove in near silence back to the cabin by the river, whose autumn roar seemed a warning, as if it might burst its banks. That *shoosh,* which I'd always so treasured, sounded terrible now. I lay there and prayed you'd be let go. The notion of your suffering a single day more overwhelmed me.

At some ungodly hour, my antique portable radio, all hum and crackle, brought me, of all things on earth, a New York cooking show, in which a chef explained at length his rules for making salmon steak with saffron and *beurre noir.* I asked myself why he or his listeners, in fact why a solitary soul should want to make that dish—or any? What, I wondered, is the point of humanity's self-deceiving, gaudy ploys, all designed to distract us from the fact of death?

Such tricks seemed pathetic. Or maybe gothic, maybe fantastic.

The mind makes its own monsters. I hadn't drunk in years. Now I half-wondered where I'd find a drink. Happily, the general store in this town of fewer than a hundred souls was closed up tight, and the town had never had a bar. These days, I couldn't wake up some old-timer, either, with whom on occasion I'd shared vanilla extract, the grandparent generation's booze of choice when the place was legally dry. Many of them continued to drink it even after the town went wet in the '70s, the vanilla habit decades in the making.

The annual Independence Day dance in the schoolhouse, the so-called Fisherman's Frolic, from which liquor was officially banned, smelled for all the world like a pastry shop, soused as it was in the sweet odor of Baker's best 80 proof. And back then there was a second store, which people called Baker's Tavern, most of its dusty shelves taken up by those small brown bottles, each of which fit handily into the back pocket of a buyer's pants.

Though it's been gone some forty years, I can see Baker's Tavern now, the wizened baloney under its scratched glass case, the outdated Wonder Bread by the register, the naked bulb that hung by a wire from the ceiling, just enough to light one's way to the juice. Right or wrong—mostly wrong, of course—I felt closer to my mentors whenever I slid some Baker's into my own hip pocket.

But my romancing alcohol for a spell that night wouldn't have gone anywhere. You hadn't approved once, and you certainly wouldn't now. I would hear your shouts of *Don't!* from within your magical cavern. You were one I'd take orders from. There haven't been that many.

The God I believe in will answer prayers, and sometimes the answer is No. Thank God. Hadn't I begged Him or Her or It for your release from this earth? And yet when we drove back to the clinic next day, you were more than merely revived; you were transformed, your color true, your precious gift of talk come back as well.

I ran into your doctor when I left the bedside for a moment to find the men's room. About to ask for an explanation, I saw him shrug. "Don't ask *me*," he said.

Jake and I sat and listened, in love as always with your retelling of tales you'd heard from your mother, father, grandparents, and all their friends. Once again, I marveled at the privilege of being with an older person as she remembered older persons remembering older persons as they remembered. If ever I've felt a sense of human continuity and perpetuity, it's been in circumstances like those. I'd remember the memories of the memories of the memories; I could pass them on to daughters and sons.

Stories must be saved if they're to save us. That is, if there's something that *can* save us, a race as benighted and headstrong as we seem to be. Like anyone, I can sometimes tend to pessimism, but sometimes too, I wonder whether some of us have been saved right along without knowing it.

On that day, you spoke of your own experiences as well, recalling your first married summer. Bill worked all day, while you fished and gathered and waited table or clerked in Paul's store. At night, you and he would sleep in bedrolls under the eaves of some camp uplake, no other place to call home, or often enough in the hull of a canoe, driven from shore by insects. This went on until autumn strode in.

And when it did, the pair of you went off to pick up potatoes in Aroostook County, where the hissing gales and the fields' rime-coated stones chopped your fingers. Still, you told us, you never starved; you'd cull a few spuds and cook them over an outdoor fire. You said they tasted like heaven at the end of a cold day.

You even remembered a period that you were usually less inclined to speak about: some years of factory work down in Massachusetts. In an era when such things were exquisitely rare, you were soon promoted over most of the men in your shop. Yet you knew you wouldn't and couldn't stay, good pay or not. You weren't bred for it, you claimed, and neither was your husband, who had a job in a rivet factory. But even down there, you recalled, "I thought of all the thousands He might've chosen to put on earth one day in 1920, and still the Lord picked me out. So I didn't fuss about things down to Waltham either."

As so often, you insisted that every day was a treasure.

I had to ask, "Even yesterday?"

You nodded. "Even that one." A pause. "Now that it's over and done."

Then I heard that belly laugh, which I've always wanted somehow to package or bottle, sure as I am that it could rescue the world. "Even that one," you repeated.

A nurse brought in a tray of food, all of it some hue of white: a scrap of haddock, mashed potatoes, milk, rice pudding. Your brow dropped slightly as you picked at it, you who could take the most unlikely stuff and cook up a banquet. Poking at the wretched excuse for a fish, you recounted how you and Bill came home sometimes and dumped a mess of brook trout into the washtub, cleaned them together, dredged them in flour, and fried them in bacon fat. "If there's heaven," you whispered, "there'll be a trout for dinner."

I hope you are eating trout.

As we sat there, I knew that murderers and crooks, monsters of public office and corporate boardroom and academic faculty, were plying their trades, telling lie after lie, drunk on their own greed or lust for dominion. I was happy you stood—sometimes, it seemed, all by yourself—against *that* sort of appetite.

You're gone, though never, to drag in one last hackneyed locution, from the hearts of those you touched and taught. I think of you each day, but now, recording all this, I suddenly have it in mind to catch a fish somewhere, if only in my imagination. I'll find a brook trout, the lovely creature that used to swim our streams in their plenty. I never keep a game fish of any sort nowadays. I release everything, but in this case I mean to make an exception. I'll net that trout and fetch it home and dress it. Then, that radio cook's recipe long forgotten, I'll stir the wood fire, frazzle some bacon, lay the fish in the cast-iron pan.

That open North lives on, my queen, my goddess. The river's call is as constant as constant can be. I'll eat what I cook. I'll finish it all. With gusto. Flake by flake.

Annie Fitch, everyone's Good Mother, with a spread of her renowned pies.

Summer

Summary

The Crossing

Last night's dream surprised me, including as it did the crossing of the Morris Road and a dirt track on the farm next to my uncle's. I hadn't seen that plot of ground in fifty years. It's likely nothing but houses there in any case today.

About half a mile down the road from the crossing, my friend Jackie and I had once stolen a stuffed owl, which we discovered in an outbuilding of another farm, moribund, down-at-heel. The place belonged to a preacher turned stumbling drunk after leaving his ministry—or being forced from it. Who cared?

We peeked through a parlor window at the old wreck, passed out in a bizarre chair with a movable lectern attached to one arm, some magazine he'd been reading sprawled open before him. Then we made for his shed and his owl.

We'd make good use of the bird. We always camped in our crow blind nights before a hunt, so it struck me as strange that, although the blind appeared in the dream, Jackie didn't. After a shoot, however successful— or more often otherwise, before we got our fabulous decoy—we'd linger, sweet bacon- and bean-smoke rising from our fire through a thick maple's leaves, a crow's corpse or two in the weeds if we'd been lucky. To dream up that maple and to smell our primitive cooking was to wake with a throb in my soul.

A black-and-white sign at the crossing read *Stop Look + Listen,* as of course we didn't. There was only one train a day, and it made its way at a rate so sluggish we liked to amble our ponies in front of it, just so we could bring on the fat engineer's mute scream through the glass of his lumbering diesel's cab.

So we flirted with death, or pretended to flirt with it anyway.

This morning in bed, I found myself wondering, What if we'd paid more attention to the wider world in those summers, the way the adult sorrows and joys of anyone's life will cause him to do? Where did we think we were going? I recall no debate, not even a conversation about such a matter. Neither one of us imagined a destination. The point was to keep on moving, whatever the day's pursuit—unless we were hiding in rapt stillness, in the blind.

At length we stole the sign. The railroads were dying even in those days, so it was never replaced, which annoyed us a little. We stashed the thing beneath the maple, face-up within the walls of brush and vine we used for camouflage.

So *Stop Look + Listen* became our table in that last summer. We felt proud of our contrivance, proud to be clever thieves, or smart alecks, as my uncle's hired man called us, "smart" something different to us from what he meant. To us it signified young, superior to others, whether we traveled horseback or hunkered under our tree, motionless, except when we blew on our crow calls, then cupped ears to hear a response from some farther field.

A response was sure to come. All that we wanted would come.

I hadn't missed Jackie so much in decades as when I woke.

The engineer's furious expression was a constant in those few years, whenever we moseyed the ponies before his train. Why should his help-less rage have delighted us so? Why did we love to see him shoot up both his middle fingers in their idiot thick striped gloves? Of course we'd answer him double, four digits to his paltry two.

We didn't care where those trains were headed, where they were coming from. Did the driver have a wife? If so, did he and she have chil-dren? We never guessed at these things either, I'm certain.

What if a pony had stumbled? Disaster. But the pony wouldn't; such a thing was impossible.

Not so many years later, Jackie did die, his Harley careening wildly through another intersection in another time. But in the time I summon here, we must have imagined that no one could come to harm at the crossing. We couldn't picture a future less hospitable than the present we savored. No child is cursed with that sort of foresight.

Intoxicated by our own ingenuity, we rigged a string from our stuffed owl back to the blind. We could pull that cord so the owl bowed. The effect was clumsy, unnatural, but for all the crows' fabled intelligence, we could shoot our barrels hot at them, at least for long minutes. We could play at annihilation.

No, I'd never have dreamed Jackie gone, or any other misfortune. No dead loved ones. No heartsickness for the sorrows, great and small, in wife or child of my own. We were merely keeping our own lives lively, oblivious of others. We were dodging mothers and fathers, importunate brothers and sisters, the tedious school-day year, the standstill culture of the suburbs, which encroached on the farm and devoured it for good shortly after I left for upper New England.

The only adult we respected was my fiery uncle himself, though that respect was as self-serving as all our other values. He called the crows *corn-thieving bastards,* which gave us a rationale for our witless destructions.

We jeered the engineer with his upthrust fingers. We jeered that judgmental hired man, nuts as he was for religion. He couldn't string ten words together without folding in some snippet of Holy Writ, which seemed to make his talk a patchwork of contradiction. *Don't hide your light under a bushel,* he'd advise us, quickly following up with *The first shall be last,* which he took to mean—or which we took him to mean—that we were no better than anyone else, and if we thought we were, time was coming when we'd learn the truth.

But then wasn't the truth supposed to make us free? Didn't he say that too?

Old folks, we thought, were more than mixed up; they were end-lessly repetitious. They were always insisting that Jackie and I be humble, that we stop and look things over. They were always so damned cautious. Why would we bother to listen?

Now Jackie's long dead, and here I am, having ridden up to the old folks' ages, and past.

Brown, Gilbey's, Happy Ending

I recall a time when, like many another hyper-hormonal young man, and in fact like too many anglers even now, I yearned to smack a big trout over the head on every outing. You can take a picture with your cell phone today, though I hope that you leave such a contraption home when you head for the river, but in those days you released the little ones and kept the whoppers, because what peer would credit your conquests on the strength of your lying word alone?

Ego, as will be shown, is this story's anti-hero.

It was 1970. I'd traveled to the Green River in Wyoming, precisely to gather some bragging rights, even if all I'd have on return would be, precisely, my word about some titan stretched halfway along my rod. I didn't own a camera, still don't.

I'd scheduled six days on the water, and almost before I knew it, five had vanished. I'd caught a fair number of fish in that span, some perhaps in the two-pound range, but none that answered to the fantasies I'd concocted back in New England. On this final day, I felt as desperate as determined, though the urgency had very likely been there from the start of the trip. It was a character flaw of mine never to be quite satisfied; I've striven to check that defect in later life, though old habits die hard.

If as aspirant author I took some reassurance from Paul Valéry's assertion that poems are never finished, only abandoned, still deep inside me I longed to compose an epic. A couple two-pounders had been fine . . . well, no they hadn't. I was working on some *fishing* epic, and four decades ago I persuaded myself that my visionary Green River trout would bring it to completion, at least for a time.

That final September morning broke into bone-numbing cold. It was snowing—not a lot, but surely snowing—and the north wind blew hard enough to sweep away such blue wings and midges as hatched at all.

Like most people who use a fly rod, I take my greater pleasure in fishing to a rise, but I've never been some dry fly purist. And so, long johns under my waders, a coarse wool sweater under my vest, I set out to swing a streamer or drift a nymph, or rather to throw all manner of each until I'd exhausted my supply and my zeal. Before that point came, I hoped I'd lay into my monster, preferably a brown, the fish that was for me, as now, a paragon. Hell, I rationalized, he was likely too big to bother with some piddling surface bug anyhow.

The water in my chosen stretch looked placid, but it had the authority of massive, slow-moving things. Elephant. Ox. Draft horse. I leaned upstream and tied on a streamer. Careful not to give any fly short shrift, I made scores of casts with each in my wallet—Muddler, Matuka, Ranger, various leech patterns, even a wretched Hornberg, in which I'd never had faith and still don't. On and on and on, and each a loser. I even tossed an Atlantic salmon fly or two, just to say I'd tried everything.

Out came the nymph box, or boxes: Prince, Copper John, Hare's Ear, Art Flick's deadly Stone Creeper, and more lethal still, at least in the east, a thing that I and the postmaster of Peru, Vermont, the best trout fisherman I knew in those days, had thrown together from tying remnants in the prior spring. He called it the White-Ass Baboon: mallard quill thorax ribbed in gold wire ahead of roughened white hare dubbing, no wing. *Nada.*

After four hours of such *nada,* I staggered up to the local eatery to warm myself and grab a bite. The counterman suggested what he called an Eye-talian sandwich, its foam-like roll soggy with tomato ooze and oil. It tasted delicious somehow, even if in my lust to go back wading I all but inhaled the thing. I decided to pick up a quart of Gilbey's gin too, for celebration of the big fish I'd be lugging to camp. I had no way to cook such a catch or freeze it, but I'd worry about that when the time came.

Wind and snow had not abated during my mealtime layoff. At one point, having gone back to streamers in the gale, I managed to stick a number 10 hook through my cheek. It didn't hurt at first. In fact I imagined I'd snagged some part of my clothing, and only after running my hand up the leader did I find the trouble. There was pain enough, all right, when I pushed the barb through and twisted at it with my nippers until the steel at last fell apart.

Blood from the wound dribbled onto my vest and ratty sweater. It struck me how surprisingly little of it I'd parted with. Anyhow, my principal soreness lay in losing half an hour of fishing to that crude doctoring.

I ran the alpha to omega of the fly assortment all over again, astounded that nothing better than 13 inches could be the result. Rather than my best day, this one was rapidly proving my worst of the trip. I'd waded up and down that vast run for a quarter mile or more in each direction, even venturing into scarily heavy water at its tail, where my fly raced through a full swing almost the moment I dropped it. I wasn't settling for halfway effort.

I sensed the invisible sun bleakly sinking behind me. Time for something radical. I remembered the Batten Kill on chilly autumn mornings in Vermont, when the spawning browns of that blessed era would sometimes rise to a spider if we skittered it over the surface. Nine out of ten times, a fish would merely slap its tail near the fly—and once only. He'd never come again after that first whack. Yet every so often, in a flurry of froth, a decent one would gulp the spider. Then the contest, usually in the brown's favor, would be on.

I tapered my tippet to 6x, blew on my fingertips, tied on a cinnamon spider, then flung it onto the river just anyhow. Twitching it a few times, I gasped as a gigantic head showed behind it. The trout did not slap at the fly like those New England browns; he merely rose in all his pomp, then sank easily back.

My heart sped and lagged in the same moment. My lunker had presented himself, but that would be the last I'd see of him if past experience were a gauge. Nonetheless, wind behind me, I made a roll cast, flicked the spider back and forth to dry, and set it down right where I had.

The brown sipped the fly like a Trico. Then, in the manner of real trophy fish, rather than roaring off, he sulked in the streambed, shaking his head for what seemed a long time. Next he made a brutal but very short run, gave a few more shakes, and swam deliberately upstream.

Then he took off like a bullet train.

Oh Lord, let me have him! I prayed, even though I was a more godless young man than I am an old.

I'm surely not the only fishermen who can testify to feeling mixed excitement and dread when a truly big fish takes. Thrilled to have a trophy on your line, you know it's at least even odds that the trophy will overmatch you. The brown leapt once like a rainbow, tail-walked a couple of times along the surface, then tore off in whatever direction he chose, one breathtaking run taking him almost halfway across the vast reach.

Even allowing for the exaggerative power of recall, I don't believe I've been into a trout of such bulk again except perhaps in Alaska, and there I was fishing a ten-pound test, level leader. Of course, I don't fish a fraction as much as I did before any of my five kids was born, back when fishing seemed both to define and validate my very existence during the warmer months. I certainly hadn't tied into such a monster before.

I've taken my share of fine ones since, but although for well over a quarter-century I have kept none, I've profoundly savored playing each before release. And in later years I have all but equally relished fighting fish that in the end broke or pulled off. To know the creature was there seems wonder enough, and pleasure.

Things were different back then. Nothing remotely like pleasure informed my battle with this particular brown. I grimly chased him up- and downriver. Tippet material not what it is now, when, as my friend Landy Bartlett once quipped, you can practically tow a truck around with 6x, I took care not to let him get too tight on me, and I kept at my fatuous pagan prayer the whole while: *Please, please, God!*

How much time ran by as I matched wits and strength with that dream fish? I haven't any idea, but a good deal, I'd bet. At last, he started coming my way. I still let him go when he wanted, but the runs were becoming less lordly.

Traveling light, I'd brought along one of those nets you twist and fit into a holster on your belt. Holding the rod tip high with my right hand, I pulled the thing out, dipped it to open the bag, and gently lifted under Leviathan—who, too long and heavy for such a contraption, collapsed the frame and wallowed again at my feet.

I made four or five further efforts with the flimsy net, terrified that each would mark the moment of escape. Then I looked downstream to those daunting rips. Just above them, a gravel beach sloped up at a gentle angle. To haul my trophy onto that beach seemed my only recourse, risky as it was, because once the brown made his way to the white water, he'd be gone.

By now, I was nearly dragging the poor brute, a matter that didn't concern me as it would today. Indeed, I checked behind myself periodically to see if the trout had turned onto its side, so that I could just pinch him under the gill plates and *carry* him out.

At last I backed two or three feet onto the sand, reeled the butt of my leader through the top guide, and lifted. *Nada.*

I didn't know what to make of this until I noticed the brown sidling offshore to fin in the pebbled shallows. Its dorsal broke the surface. I saw the little pigtail at my tippet's end, which now trailed useless below me. I had obviously tied a bad knot with my frozen fingers.

I dropped my rod on the beach, waded out to the trout's lie, and swiped at him like a grizzly bear. An inept bear at that: when the water cleared, I watched my trophy drift backwards ever so slowly. Then, with one flick of his tail, he disappeared.

What swam to mind then was not another fish but that bottle of Gilbey's in my pack. This would become a more and more common response as I went on in life.

The Wind River Mountains, however cloaked in mist and snow, provided a sight to make the hike back to my cabin worth the taking. Mule deer and antelope grazed in the meadows, breaths visible in the cold when they raised their heads. More than one golden eagle circled above. The sage showed the spectral green that would tax a Corot to replicate. But that foggy-glassed bottle of gin was the focus of my mind's eye.

When I got indoors, the bottle's contents vanished, and a good deal faster than my trout had. So did the rest of that day and night as I drowned my defeat. But had I netted the trout, I'd have toasted my triumph to the limit and beyond. There was always some motive for that first belt, after which who knew what was coming?

I woke up next morning to wonder where in hell I might be, and what in hell I'd been doing to take myself there. Having fallen asleep in my damp clothing, waders and all, and having left the radio on, I slowly recognized Hank Williams's "Your Cheatin' Heart," performed by someone who was no Hank Williams. I lolled and shivered.

I pinch myself today to think that, memory finally prevailing, my failure on the Green soon led me to think that life had no value for me anymore, that nothing—nothing!—could ever again come right. I had not merely lost the best trout I'd ever had on a line; I'd lost the world. Insane, of course, but then addiction and insanity are close kin.

Forehead in hands, elbows on knees, quaking like a whippet, I began to feel as though some poisonous worm were boring inside my skull. The pain in my head was largely hangover, but it seemed too that my worm had fangs, that I could all but watch it sink them into what remained of my brain.

Too many years would pass before that worm, some avatar of conscience, I suppose, gnawed all the way through my pride, sat me flat on a floor in Vermont, and broke me but good. I would quit drinking or die. Things struck me just that simply and rightly. I thank God for the moment of clarity.

Today, when my heart and soul are at peace, which is most of the time, I am open to quotidian miracles. I sometimes notice, say, a crab apple tree dripping exotic, resplendent foliage, which turns out to be a flock of waxwings. At other times, I'm struck by how the ramshackle veneer mill in the town just south of ours is inverted and beautified by the calm water of the mill stream below it. Crystals hovering in the subzero air as I snowshoe through an opening in woods can rob my breath. I don't mind platitude here: these are some things that feed what I now name my soul, lend it a measure of strength.

At that moment by the Green, I had no means to imagine any of this, none to foresee how I'd thrive on family ties and treasured friendships and what, just half-jokingly, I now call "good, clean fun."

It has taken every day I've lived to get me to where I am now.

I'm nurtured as well, and more surprisingly, by what remains of that very trip to the Green, the one I believed such a botch. I can re-envision the haloed crimson spots along the flanks of my fabled fish, his deep but streamlined shape. Snowflakes hit the surface to vanish immediately. Stones glimmer on the river-bottom. I find poignant beauty in all such transitory things. And if in mind I lift my eyes to the hills, as I must after all have done back then, I see the whited coulees descend the Wind Rivers like angel-pale lava, wild grazing animals lit by the shine.

It was my subconscious, or some other ineffable faculty, that stored up these gleanings until they could properly impress themselves on my spirit. And here they are, bright and compelling enough to be parts of this story's happy ending.

Daybook, July

I've recently been reading one of my favorite writers on the American West. Ted Leeson is a master of lyrical prose and perhaps above all of meditation on place. Today I came across an opinion in his superb *Inventing Montana* that struck me as vividly as when I first saw it.

"Montana," Ted asserts, "is not a place. It is merely the name of a place, a convenience of language."

That got me to thinking, scarcely for the first time, about the places in my own work. But not the places only. The experiences and events and above all the people with whom I've dealt both in my nonfiction and perhaps above all in my poetry, which tends toward the nonfictional too, are or were all real. No doubt about that in my mind. Once I've put them on the written page, or even spoken of them aloud, however, they become . . . what?

I found myself wondering about something that so many of my hundreds and hundreds of students—usually in defense of their own poetry or fiction at its least cogent—often called Things That Really Happened. Were my work's components, human and otherwise, largely concocted? Did I impose an identity upon them and in that measure "invent" them? Were they what Ted calls conveniences of language?

Anything other than truth, I believed, would be an insult to the cherished folks and locations I've meant to praise. But damned if truth isn't a troublesome issue.

I recall reading the words of a Native American woman –Kiowa, I believe—who was called as a witness in a criminal trial. When asked to tell the whole truth, she replied, "I don't know the whole truth; I only know what I know." The world would be the better for more of such modest knowledge, for even the notion of knowledge itself is a troublesome one.

Not that I am particularly interested in all this as a *philosophical* issue. Fact is, I am often rather suspicious of philosophy, the more formal, the more suspicious. Of course much of my aversion must be based on my ineptitude at abstract thought.

If I can't immediately integrate something with my personal experience, I'm not likely to understand it, or if I do, to retain it.

I'm aware of the human tendency, from which I am scarcely immune, to present what one can do as an asset and what one can't as a defect. However all this may be, though, I long since decided that literature made a better vehicle for me to contemplate the world than what the philosophers could offer. Creative approaches (though I rather despise that adjective, especially as in the despicable recent coinage, *creative nonfiction*) seem more accurately to grapple with the complexity and the contradictoriness of my experience than other means.

When handled by a master, which I don't claim to be, art can entertain a whole gaggle of ideas, despite the fact that, at least superficially, one of those ideas may run directly counter to another, that one to yet another, and so on.

John Keats spoke of "Negative Capability," the capacity to be "in Mysteries, uncertainties and doubts, without any irritable reaching after fact and reason." I have always taken this to mean that the verbal artist can, to choose the most radical and convenient example, simultaneously consider the world's horrors and the world's blessings, and, even more stunningly, can demonstrate how one is often an aspect of the other. Logic probably doesn't like all this multifariousness, but I don't believe the great universe gives a damn about logic's affections or disaffections. I know I don't.

Outside my window now, I see two dapper kingfishers flitting at the edges of our pond, their feathers shocking light. Despite a morning fog, October's trees show equally bright. But my reader can't tell, as I testify to this, whether the birds and the trees shine in this way because they actually shine in this way or because just now I've imagined a break in the mist through which a sun is pouring, so sharp it could make you bleed.

One day in 2009, seven lithe otters led me, my brother Jake, and our friend Landy downstream as we fished the mighty Missouri. That's a memory of Ted's Montana, a place either real or imaginary. Truth is, I think, it's both. The otters were there, right enough, and there were too many for them to be a mother animal and her brood. Still, that *was* the number, seven. I didn't have to come up with it.

But I might have if I'd needed to.

Seven, I'd recall, has often been a mystical number, which would seem more than handy, because the seven-ness of that crowd of otters seemed consistent, precisely, with the mystical aura they had. Or that I lent them. Or at least lend them now. They were, from what's maybe a clearer point of view, just water creatures, better suited to such a milieu than the three of us, casting our fabricated carbon-compound fly rods, moving downstream in our Kevlar boat.

And I think of another water scene when I watched an eagle as he stooped on a Canada goose. It surely couldn't have been a figment. I'd been paddling a kayak north from my town in Vermont, cleaving close to the eastern, New Hampshire bank of the river, staying under the cottonwood and silver maple canopy, out of the hard sun. I was training for a race in August.

Just as I rounded a bend, I watched the big raptor, with talons flared, hit the goose's neck, *smack!* That goose collapsed on the sand beach, as suddenly dead and motionless as if I'd shot it myself with the old Browning Lightning I carried back when I hunted near there for waterfowl.

Didn't I hunt there? Of course I did.

I intended to stop and watch the eagle, whose tail showed dark stripes, which meant a young bird. Or at least I prefer him young, though I'm not certain why, nor why I prefer him to be *him*. I meant to pause, to hell with the workout, with an eye to beholding another dive from the blighted elm, to which the predator had retreated on noticing me. Maybe it wasn't an elm, or even diseased, but again, I want this to be so. And I need the elm to lean at the proper angle.

But no: these were actual observations.

For the moment, a plan in mind, I kept on moving northward, amid a score or so of early fallen leaves, umber and mauve, that floated upriver, counter to nature. We were a long way from autumn, yet I'm sure those leaves floated there. I'm less sure that *umber* and *mauve* really correspond to the leaves' real colors. The words do sound lovely, however, even in my own ears—maybe there especially. It's a problem.

You may imagine that I've also invented that illogical upriver drift of boat and leaf, but, trust me, I know this river like the proverbial back of my hand, spending some seventy or eighty days on it in the warmer months. I've even paddled here in February when the water stayed open. Things were moving upstream simply because right at that turn there's a big eddy. I was carried along by its backwash, just like those leaves.

To be on the Connecticut River, at least the part that's handiest to where I live, constitutes more than a mere pleasure for me; it creates a certain state—not *Vermont,* not *New Hampshire,* not *border.* It is more, if you'll allow me, a state of mind, even if over there stand the irrefutable mountains, especially that genuine massif, Moosilauke. Those summits loom off eastward, though the river-course is so sinuous that Black Mountain, for example, seems to come at a paddler from a different angle in every minute, as if it really could change position.

I planned to stay waterborne for as long as muscle and will prevailed, and I did, but first, as I say, I rode that eddy around the bend and upriver for fifty yards or so. Then, pulling even closer to the New Hampshire shore to avoid the backwash and to keep myself covered, I drifted down to spy on the eagle, which must have swooped back to his kill once I passed onward.

But he hadn't. Or at least I don't think so. The goose lay there, great lump, looking as big, almost, as calf or burro. I squinted. That mound *was* the goose, no? I couldn't find its killer in tree or sky.

I put my blades back in and pulled another three miles against the current before I turned around and followed it back. So it was more than an hour before I rode past the spot again. I drew my boat up on the sand and stepped across it.

Nothing remained but a spine. Even the wings and scaly feet were gone.

This, I reasoned, was a graphic illustration of wildlife economy, because it hadn't been the eagle alone to gorge on that corpse. Tracks of turtles and ravens and even tiny rodents also showed in the sand. But with only the remnant backbone to go on—a knobby column that might have been there for years, no sign of fresh blood upon it—could I prove, even, or especially, to myself, that the goose had ever existed, let alone that I'd witnessed its murder, so ugly and beautiful, so terrifying and graceful?

I blinked at the chain of vertebrae. I blinked at the dead-standing tree to which the eagle had retreated. I blinked at the mountains. I felt a little light-headed. Maybe what I had seen was a phantasm, an aggregate of a hundred disparate memories on this stream.

There are dogs I've treasured, quick and lost; there are horses and songs; there are people, living and gone, who have figured into my life, which has been, in so many ways, for all my physical and mental exertions among woods and waters, a life of words, an extended story.

I have tried to portray living creatures and their environs and productions in an imaginative way, yes, but whatever I've talked about is fact. It has to be true. Otherwise, all I had were some maps. I had no places. It has to be true. Otherwise, I never knew old woodsmen and their tales. I merely read a few books, some of them my own. I had nothing. I never knew a soul, a thing.

I can't tell you why, when I got back into my kayak, I decided to coast it upstream again for a spell, borne by the same eddy's current. I suppose I liked the feel of being borne north on south-flowing water. I liked sensing the river as it moved me—as some of my visions do, including those of Things that Really Happened—in a way that suggested my up could be my down, my progress against a flow could be that fluent, that easy, at least for moments.

Living with the Stories

In August of 1993, his eighty-eighth on earth, I asked Earl Bonness down to my river camp and turned on a battery-powered tape recorder, old-fashioned even for the time, purchased when the camp itself was in 1968. I'd mentioned the man here and there in various writings, but I wanted to present him more fully. Earl was after all a living hero of mine, among the last of a certain upper New England kind; he needed his own chapter. There were countless reasons to turn to him, but one was that all the other heroes—at least the male ones—had about gone by the time of our conversation.

Earl's chapter, I imagined, would be founded on that dialogue, but I would add to it a tribute, the best I could manage. When I played the tape back, however, it was as always Earl's own voice that moved me. His words blended with the steady rush of the river outdoors, so that at length I thought of that odd but majestic figure in Saint John's Revelation: the Ancient of Days. Who spoke with the voice of many waters. Who saw the beginning and the ending of a world. In these respects Earl, a river driver in the more fabulous period of lumberjacking, the time, precisely, of the waters, speaks apocalyptically too, and no author's testimony to his life and vision could improve on the one he provides on his own.

If, therefore, I first decided to let the old man's voice simply flow (the verb is inevitable), I subsequently decided against impeding that fluidity, against imposing any shapeliness beyond the implicit, associative one contained in the musings that follow, unedited. In short, I deleted all of my trivial parts in the conversation.

My chief regret is that the sonorities and rhythms of Earl's out-loud talk cannot be captured in print.

Let him begin:

I went on my first drive in 1925, over on the Machias River. The job took forty-two days. First we drove what's called Old Stream, and drove it to the end. There was prime logs so big we couldn't ford them into the main river, and I imagine some are laying on the bank right now. We moved from there to the Mopang, which is another tributary of the Machias, and we drove that in too. Less of a business, because there were a little more water. Mopang had a dam, and we could build up a head before we sent our wood.

When we got done with Old Stream and the Mopang, we took for Third Machias Lake, where an old fella from Wesley named Jim McLean had cut a million board feet in the eastern arm. That put us back to a tough job, getting the booms out of there and down through the islands. You know them islands: pretty as a picture to look at, but oh my! Finally we made it, and we sluiced the timber, and followed those logs a month and a half till we come into Whitneyville, down on the coast. That was the end of our drive.

There lived a family name of Sullivan in that town, very wealthy, because they'd sold a lot of land to St. Regis, which is Champion International now. Folks said the Sullivans was worth a million dollars, and that meant money in those days. That was really money. But still one old Sullivan was left who kept on running a store.

This particular Mr. Sullivan and his wife had a tame bear: oh, a big old brute, but you could pat him on the head like a dog. Well, the storekeeper told us how he arrived at him. You see, there was a bounty on bear. I'm not claiming there should have been, but there it was. And one day a fella comes in lugging a cub he found by the side of the road, because someone apparently killed his mother. And this Sullivan says right off, "Take him out." But his wife meant to contradict him: "We'll keep the bear." Was that like a woman? Tender-hearted.

Well, the first year they built him a yard and a house and made a great pet of him. When it came November, though, he wouldn't eat. And they was nervous over it, being fond of him by then. They didn't have any help, and the animal seemed like a fine companion. An old trapper came in, and he said, "There's nothing wrong with your bear. Put some straw in his house. He wants to go to sleep, is all." They done it, and sure enough he got through the winter.

By the next fall he was grown into quite a junk of a bear, and as I say they'd made a great friend of him. But somehow the missus knew something, and she said to her husband, "He's getting restless. Go out and put on his collar." Old Sullivan done what she asked. He was a nice man. But come morning, the bear had slipped that collar. Gone. And Mr. Sullivan told her, "It's just as well. He's better off in the wild." You see, I keep talking about how dear the beast was to these folks, but the old fella—truth is, he wasn't all that attached.

The following April commenced unusual warm. Mr. Sullivan took to sleeping in a downstairs bedroom to keep an eye on the goods, because the windows was open. He told me that in the middle of the night he became conscious of a great weight upon him. He reached down and fetched up two hands full of hair. The bear was laying right across him. Came in one of them windows.

You know what the old guy said? "Earl," he said, "that was one of life's darkest moments." After being gone so long in the woods, who knew but the bear turned ugly? But this Sullivan prayed a little, I imagine, and then he rolled the bear off the bed, took him out to the yard and put that collar back on again. And the wife, my, she was really happy about her bear being back again. But I'll tell you: that was really a story.

And that bear never went back to the woods.

In my time, I have shot and trapped more bear than I want to speak of. The last one I caught was a female, and I had to shoot her because she put up such a fight. I got remorseful, and I told my wife that evening, "I'll never set the trap again," and I didn't. A few years ago I sold that trap for $150. 1 paid sixty when I bought it. Of course, it's a monstrous thing, you know, big enough that you have to set it with clamps. But I got so sick from watching that old bear fight as hard as she did.

That river drive was a mighty tough job, if you want me to be honest. We worked practically all the daylight there were. An old man cooked for thirty-eight other men over an open fire, and he had three cookees, which dried the pans and dishes by sticking all of them in a flour sack and working them back and forth. By golly, that cook was quite a man. Charlie Rogers. I remember him well. I did like him.

Well, I liked most of the men in that crew. I got on with them all. There wasn't any brawling or fighting. You had to get along. I weighed 195 pounds or so in them days, pretty rugged. But there was no trouble. We worked hard enough to keep us tamed down pretty good. We all worked hard, downriver or back home, and we used each other in a proper way.

Don't let me say there was never any hard feelings of any kind, but a lot of them comical too. I'll tell you a story, true one. We had a fella in these parts back then, Jim Bacon. He lived out on Tough End, same as I do, and he was a character. There came a peddler with a horse and wagon about twice a month—Reuben, the peddler. He had different things for sale in his cart, but mostly clothes. And he was up to the Grand Lake landing when Jim and I came in from guiding one evening and pulled up our canoes.

Now Jim's pants was bedraggled somewhat, so he went over and said, "Reuben, you got pants? I need some." Reuben told him yes, and Jim sorted through till he found a pair that'd do him. We were paid five dollars a day as guides then, so when he asked Reuben his price, and when Reuben told him four dollars, why, Jim looked around and said "God almighty, I'd sell everything I own for four dollars! Moccasins, hat and all."

Reuben says, "Take 'em off."

They bargained pretty near till dark before Jim agreed to sell everything he had on but his union suit. He got down Middlewalk by the canal without seeing anyone, but at the bridge who does he meet but Agnes Yates? Now Agnes, she had a tongue like no one you ever heard. She pointed a finger at him and said, "Jim Bacon, somebody ought to shoot you." And Jim looked back over at her and said, "You know something, Agnes? If you was my wife, I'd save them the trouble."

Now these are stories, aren't they? We could remember them all. Still can. It's a changed world. We told stories. We lived with stories.

Now they was going to have a parade this last Independence with what was left of us old guides. Damn few. They meant to haul us in a wagon. What would be your opinion of that? Well, it's no matter, because the day was rainy and they never had their show.

Of course there's TV and all that now. That's not the same as stories.

But I admit there were sides of those old days I speak of that was grim. Quite grim. There's always that, I guess. I had a great friend in Creston MacArthur. He was maybe thirteen years old when I moved over to Tough End in 1932. He came by a lot, right till he died a few years back. A nice guy, good-hearted, help you out any time he could. And you know, I miss him something awful. I bet you do too, Syd. Anybody would.

Life is full of sadness. We lost a daughter, our youngest one. She was away at school at the time. She was sixteen. And then our oldest son. He come back from Vietnam after that war was over, and he'd had a lot of training in heavy equipment. He found a job at Georgia Pacific, and he still works for the same outfit. He got himself married, and by and by him and her didn't get along all that well. So one day his wife brought our grandson Tommy over and left him. He was two years old. She gave him to Tecky. My wife's real name is Thelma, but her family was from County Clare and very Irish and that's what they called her and everyone still does.

Doggone it, we raised that child. He grew into quite a boy. Finally he got work in the mill in Woodland and boarded there. No car. He and some others was looking over guns, and they called it suicide. It wasn't suicide. One of them guns went off and killed him. And you live with those things. It's never easy. He was a nice boy. He could cast a fly pretty good. Of course, he had a lot of practice on the stream here. The stream's not what it was, naturally. I caught a couple this spring. They was filled out nice, but I let them go. I didn't need them.

Yes, you tell a lot of stories, but memories will bear down on you. When people talk about the days before the changes, sometimes you'd think it was heaven on earth. But yes, we did have stories, you want to believe. Enough to go around. You take Warren Berry, an old timer like me. Gone now. Warren and I got together when they built the naval base down in Machias. Carpenters. Our main job was finishing off the Quonset huts for the personnel to live in.

One day we traveled out to visit a fella in East Machias who was a friend of Warren's, because Warren was raised in that town. This man's name was Freddie McGeorge, and he had a mill there, a sawmill. Freddie told us of how one morning, when something was bothering in the mill, he went to the phone, the old kind hanging on the wall, which you cranked up. He got the operator and she kept saying, "I can't understand you, Mr. McGeorge, I can't understand you." So finally Freddie got a little ugly and he said, "Well, Jesus H. Christ! There, did you understand that?"

Now this operator didn't like it. She told him, "Mr. McGeorge, you cannot use profanity on the telephone. I'm going to send a fellow up to take your speaker out." He said, "You can do it, and then stuff it up your butt." Oh, he had a temper.

Well, the man came to take the phone away. Mr. McGeorge said, "I'll make one more call before you start in," and the man said that would be all right. He got the operator again, and she said to him: "Oh, Mr. McGeorge, I'm so happy you called me to apologize." He said, "Lady, I didn't call for that. That fella's here after the phone, so you best get your drawers down."

By and by, of course, Warren and I came home to go guiding, which I done for seventy years. Today I don't take anyone except for one old party—oh, maybe two or three—which I've had for a very long time. All I have now is what they call an honorary guide's license, you see, so I don't tie on to too much.

The fishing's not a shadow of what it was anyhow, and won't ever be again. But in the thirties, the Depression years across the country . . . well, a person *needed* a fish. Hadn't have been for them, and raising a garden—well, folks would've had a mighty tough go.

In the forties, things was picking up again and I was guiding a couple. They looked around and saw how beautiful everything was. Don't know why I remember them special; they called it so pretty, and by God it still is. Five dollars a day, though, and a long day too. And now it's a hundred and twenty. I went to a meeting when it was still a hundred and I told the young guides they weren't going to get so many parties, they were going to overprice their business. And they said, Oh no, they had to have another twenty dollars on top, which was a mistake. That was a mistake. I said, "Boys, go ahead, it don't mean a thing to me. My days are gone." But these young fellas thought that was the thing to do and they done it.

Well, I guess, why not? I want to tell you, though, I think we might've been better neighbors when we had less money. Seems so anyhow.

But I was telling you about this couple in the forties. I guided them very frequently and for many years. Now the woman looked about—it was a wonderful day, all right—and she commented on how it appeared. But she was a long way from a fool, and she asked me, "Earl, were you poor in the Depression years?" I said, "Missus, everybody was poor, not just me. But I can let you know just how poor I was. I had a hound that oftentimes got so weak from hunger he had to lean agin a bank to bark." She said, "You'll never change." And I don't know but she was right. She's gone on too.

Times get better, but you look back on the old days and the old-timers. We'd be guiding together, sometimes two, maybe three of us to a party, and everything was peaceful. However, I went down about a year ago to what they call the Lynn Farm on the west bank of the St. Croix River. We caught some fairly good fish, and when it came time for lunch, I pulled us onto what's known as Birch Rips Island, after the rips that was there back when we sluiced logs in that country.

One young fella said, "Well, you don't know as you have permission to lunch here, and it's a private island." I said, "I know the lady that owns it." And for some reason that just made him cross somehow. "Oh," he looks at me and says, "you're always right, ain't you?" I told him, "Well, on this particular occasion I do happen to be right." You wouldn't call that conversation. But I guess there's no substitute for youth, and they're good boys. Some of them could do a little better sometimes. Well, who couldn't?

Maybe it's all how you're raised to conduct yourself. I came from what they call Basswood Ridge over in New Brunswick, born there, in my grandfather's home. His wife was another one out of County Clare, Ireland. And what do you suppose her maiden name was? J-O-Y. *Joy.* And she spoke of a potato famine when she was fourteen, and that was the major food of the Irish people. So over into Canada she immigrated with her parents.

Finally she came to St. Stephen, New Brunswick, and got a job housekeeping for the Eaton family in Calais. Eatons were of a big name there; they'd sold land to St. Croix Pulpwood. They lived by one of the bridges. There were four bridges in town then, not just two. She met my granddaddy because he was working in one of the mills in that part, which they called Milltown and still do. And then granddad bought his place out in New Brunswick and finally I was born there, as I mentioned.

But both of my parents were born on this side, so when the time came, when I was of an age, all I had to do was go down to Machias and declare my intentions, because Ma and Pa were from over here, and were living in Grand Lake Stream at the time, since I was five. That's how I got to be a U.S. citizen. Pretty easy.

I went to school some here in Grand Lake. A lady asked me—the same one who wanted to know was I poor in the Depression—how much schooling I had. I told her three days. She said, "Three days?" I said, "My brother got sick and I took his place." But I actually went through the grammar school. After that, a scholar had to go away to Woodland every day, which I done a year, but then I started in to work. I did this and that, and then I joined in with the drives. I made the first one when I was twenty. Twenty years old.

Another job I had was hanging boom stock. You see, down on the west river, there's big flowage areas near the dam at Grand Falls. And they had to boom the logs off, to keep the pulpwood from getting in among them stumps, because it was so costly to pull them out of there again. The fella who was the boss on the upriver work, old Bill Priestley, he said, "I don't know how you can do it." I was green. "You walk clear out about to the end of one of them sticks and you hop onto another and you ain't fallen in yet." I told him, "Give me time." Of course I had a pair of good cog boots, made by the Bass company, and I have them today in my shop. Stepped over a lot of timber, they did.

But there was a session when I got clear of the logging trade. I traveled out west, and I'll tell you how it happened. Over in New Brunswick, they had a special train they put on for volunteers who wanted to go into Manitoba and Saskatchewan, which was grain provinces, to work the harvest. We was making two dollars a day working for the pulp company, and if you weren't a chopper it was one dollar. Just one. I was a chopper, but still . . .

They didn't have the combines back in those days, but they did have the reapers and binders. They burned chaff from the fields to make their steam. We went behind and grabbed the middle strings of the sheaves and stood them butts down, with one on the side, one in the middle, and one on the other side. This they called stooking. Those stooks would dry where we left them. Then came the thrashing machine, and that machine would thrash sometimes seventy bushel a day of wheat. They thrashed some oats too.

That was Saskatchewan. Five dollars a day, and we thought that was big money, but when we got paid off by the landowners, two brothers, we headed for a poker game in the town of Moose Jaw. You already can tell me what happened: I got up at three in the morning, and all I had was my clothes and my hat and my moccasins. My friend Raymond Caldwell, why, he was in the same mess. We lost our money. All that money, gone.

Me and Raymond took a job in a grain elevator for two dollars a day. We didn't like it a particle, so we got thinking about going down in Montana, which borders on the province. We went to the immigration, and I showed them I was a U.S. citizen. Now Raymond wasn't, so they gave him quite an interrogation. He answered all the questions, though, and so they finally said, "OK, you can go." We landed in some bar that night, and we were having a beer when a gentleman came in with a hat three times bigger than mine.

He saw what we were drinking and he said, "You down on your luck some?"

I said to him, "You want to believe we are. How'd you tell?"

He told me, "Most fellas around here drink a little whiskey."

"Well," we told him, "beer'll do us, I guess."

Right then he spoke of a ranch he owned up toward the Milk River. "I could give you boys a job," he said. "The wages won't be much, but you'll get through the winter. Tell me where you're staying and I'll pick you up in the morning. We'll go by train." Sure enough, at daylight he called at the room we had, and we boarded a car.

Now did he have a ranch! Cattle, and then some more cattle. And horses. Them little broncos would kick us off just for exercise, but the men that lived there—well, they stuck on a saddle like glue. Raymond and I got a little better in time, but we pulled a lot of leather for a while, I'll tell you.

We stayed there for winter, just like our boss promised. Twenty dollars a month and our board, and if it hadn't been for a sheepskin coat I'd have caught my death. You see, I thought I'd been cold in Maine, but I hadn't. Some days out there would've froze an Eskimo in the cellar. It was the wind. By God, it took two men to hold on one man's hat! Which meant a poor chance if you was on a horse, and so we was most times.

Imagine Raymond and me—wranglers! But that's what we done. We'd drive those cows into the fenced lot and let them feed, and then come afternoon drive them out again because they'd waste more than they'd eat if you left them in. That was the procedure, every day. It was how that rancher wanted to do it, and he was smart. He was a pretty good guy too. Saved us, you could say.

But we wanted to come back home and did, even if we was all the next summer working our way. Into Canada we crossed again, finding a job here and there, till we finally boarded a grain boat over at Fort William, New Brunswick.

The second day out I got seasick. Was you ever seasick? Oh dear God, it's awful. Think you're going to die . . . and then you want to! And Raymond laughed at me; then by the Jesus within three days he took sick too. I laughed at *him* then, because I'd got over it.

We came into St. John and then found a train which brought us down to St. Stephen.

When I crossed back into Maine, I said, "I'm never going to leave this state again." Oh, I don't mean it weren't good country out there, and full of game. One old Indian told me that his people never called it Milk River. They said "River That Flows Geese," and by golly he was right about that. You couldn't see the water for the birds when they'd molt their feathers and couldn't fly.

We had Indians too, the Passamaquoddy people, which is of the Algonquins. More of them then, maybe. Different, anyhow. Did I ever show you the paddle made by Joe Mell? He was of the tribe, but part French too, as many were of their time. He was a character, old Joe. I bought that paddle from him for fifteen dollars, which was a week's pay, or pretty near. But listen: that blade was so thin you could spit right through it, still can; yet it's held up, straight as a die. You could lay a plumb line on it right now. What Joe said was to have your wood dry, *real* dry. And that remains the secret of a first class paddle. You learn these things. Better to learn them from a friend than a harder way . . . which I've also done, plenty.

When I think of Joe, I can't help thinking about old Belding Yates too. He ran a company steamboat called the *Robert H.* I have a picture of her over home. Belding used her when he handled the log drives from Wabassus into Compass and then through the Thoroughfare and on down. That crew out there would work all day and all night driving logs. They had a bateau as well, with a little old outboard on her. The *Robert H.* towed a shanty scow, and there was a cook aboard. But that cook became very ill off Coffin Point and they carried him downlake. So Belding had to cook himself. He didn't want to, but the boss said, "You cook or you go downlake too."

Well, the first thing he makes is a batch of cream of tartar biscuits, and he told me you couldn't break one, not with a hammer. So what's he do? He told me he just hid them. When the men asked him at lunchtime, he said there wasn't any, kept them out of sight.

When everyone went back out on the boom, by golly, along came a lone wolf in a canoe. Joe Mell. He said, "Belgian, you got cookie?" Belding said yes he did, and while Joe was eating of the cookies and drinking tea, Belding took and put that box of biscuits in his canoe. When Joe started away, he thanked Belding, but then he looked in this wooden box. He paddled back. "Belgian," he said, "what you want me to do with breads?" Belding told him, "Just get them the hell out of here."

You see, some will tell you otherwise, but it's my opinion we got along pretty well, white and Passamaquoddy together. When I was on that Old Stream drive, Newell Francis and I tended a station. We checked to see there was no cross logs; we kept things moving. He and I stayed in a little hunting camp, and we were making out good; every day one of the cookees would bring us our victuals, but we were pretty much on our own. We spent a lot of time as partners, you can bet, Newell and I did.

There was an unusual incident about twenty years later. I cut my foot with an axe and I had to go down to Calais Hospital. I didn't want an infection. This Indian lady came in while I was waiting. I spoke to her when she sat down, and I asked if she lived out on Dana Point. She told me no, she was from Pleasant Point. "Then you must know Newell Francis," I said. "Know him?" She had a big smile on her; I can see it now. Turned out to be Newell's sister! I mentioned working alongside him, and I asked whatever happened to him. She told me he was gone. Sad thing, I had to say. I mean we got on so. I enjoyed that man. Makes me sorry right now just to think of it. I told that woman I liked her brother very much.

That was the old Machias Lumber Company days, when I learned a little of the Indians' language. I can understand a lot more than I can say. Only the old ones speak the language anyhow among the Indians. The young ones aren't learning it, and it's not written down, I don't believe. So everything changes, good times and bad alike. You don't get anything much without losing something too, and lots of times when you guess you lost something you come up with something you didn't have before.

But I'd imagine the best times was when I got my first guide's license. Plenty of guiding then, even if wages didn't amount to much. I'd climb that highest ridge over Whitney Cove, and you could count eighteen lakes on a clear day. I'm a lucky man that I ever could take in a sight like that. A lot of water.

In wintertime I'd go back to the woods. Plenty of woods work too. Timber was king. All machines now. There's a verse:

The screech owl haunts the camp at dawn
Where the cook's tin pan woke men of brawn.

So you can see it's nothing compared to what it was. Nothing. I went to work one time for that old Machias Lumber Company, on Second Mopang Lake. Seven of us was hired in Calais, but we traveled to Machias by train, then set out from there with two teams. There was a fella in Wesley named Wilbur Day, and at the time he and his chum George McGoon were the most notorious poachers in the state of Maine. They'd put a dog on an island till the deer went to water for salvation, which the law never allowed at all.

Wilbur Day's mother and my grandmother were sisters. My granny's buried up here in the cemetery. Her name was very old-fashioned too— Vicey. Anyhow, we traveled on till we got to Wilbur's. He and his wife Millie ran an inn in that country. They had a barn too, so we put up overnight. In the morning, Millie made a wonderful breakfast, and we ate it, you bet your life, pancakes and biscuits and sausages and eggs and all.

The teams were hooking up when someone drove in the yard. You could hunt till the fifteenth day of December in those days. Legally. Wilbur and Millie had a few sportsmen staying in with them, and there was several deer hung up around the place. Along came this solitary man, driving a buggy.

Now Wilbur had one old hound named Sorry Face, saddest looking thing you ever saw, too old to harass the deer anymore. But that dog was wandering around this fella's wagon, and he was growling. Wilbur came over and said, "Get out, old Sorry Face! You et up all the deer and now you want to eat the warden." And it *was* the warden too, come in to check things over, because it's just as I say, Wilbur and that McGoon were notorious. "Get out, old Sorry Face!" Wilbur said. Then we went on ahead to Mopang.

And even the mills are changed. I did some millwork too, as I explained. One time I signed on with the St. Croix Paper Company to work in the sorting gap. You see, all these companies had their own mark on their logs; you'd make it with a stamping axe. I've done that as well in my life. We'd sort the logs as they came through, because they were all together there. And once a week we'd sluice them, according to which mill they were going to.

Yes, a lot of mills back then. I done well in that sorting gap, because I'd been a driver many times. You work on floating logs when you're young and you get so you can go wherever you want on one. I could swim, but most of those old-timers couldn't swim a stroke to save themselves.

A man had to travel some, so I bought a car back around those days, after Tecky and I were married a year or so. I'd been working in the woods or the mills or on the rivers and I was guiding too. So we got a Model A, which was quite a car of its time. No heater, though. You had to heat up a soapstone and wrap it and lay it on the floor.

Those were other days. But then again, we made out. I think we were more thankful for what we had than people today. They will grasp for more, but we were grateful for what we did have, even a soapstone when it was wintertime.

But I liked all the seasons. We took them as they came along. Fall was hunting, by God, you said it. Old George Bagley lived on Tough End next door to me. Quite a man, turned his hand to anything, had that shop right by his house. Well, deer was plentiful, and it was the autumn, so George came over and sat on a bench in my yard. He said, "Let's go get a deer in the burn. Lots of apples down there." I told him, "We'll do it."

On the way we jumped a few, but nobody got a shot till we separated and I moved a pair. I couldn't get a look, but they went over by George and he killed a spikehorn. We dressed him very careful, paunched him, wiped away all the blood we could with dry leaves.

I said, "I'll lug him," and I did. By and by we got abreast of Big Falls, and I needed a breather. This wasn't a heavy deer, but the walking wasn't easy in that old burn; a good charge of young brush, you see. So we sat down for a smoke. George's hearing was a little impaired, but I heard a dog after we stopped. It was Bobby Gardner's. God bless him, he just wouldn't keep them dogs at home.

Pretty soon a deer came by, but we didn't need him, and we never lifted a barrel. But when the dog came on his trail, he waited a moment looking at us, and George said, "That's no good." So I put a bead on him. We both did. I had a .44-40 rifle from my uncle; George had a .45-70. The dog started down the road and we both stood up and fired. George turned to me and said, "Either I'm as good a shot as I ever was or you're getting better."

People might not like that story. *I* don't like it. But you know, we counted on the deer, and dogs in the woods was a great menace. We told Bobby so many times and he paid it all no mind. No one knew what George and I done that day; we just buried the poor hound right there. I didn't mind people dogging deer for food, but they wanted to keep their dogs home when they wasn't using them.

It was a time of these stories, when they all got started and when we told them. Us fellas did that back then, so we had a very large assortment of them. I remember a comical incident. It was when George MacArthur and I were sitting by the company store. A big car came in that day, and by the Jesus out jumped a chauffeur, suit and all. He started asking where he could find a mechanic.

"How about you?" he asked George. "You aren't a mechanic?"

"No, sir," said George, "I'm a MacArthur."

I remember Earl Brown was there too, and him and I took to laughing! "No, sir, I'm a MacArthur, not a mechanic." That was George, all right, quick-witted.

The other fella, Earl Brown, he was a great big rugged cuss. Nice man, too. I guided with him and worked together with him in the woods. Once we came back from Princeton, Earl and I and Glenn MacArthur, George's brother. There was a beer room down there, just to be sociable, because that woman's beer was something terrific; I can't tell you how bad it tasted. So this particular evening we happened to purchase a small jar of something better, you see. On the way home we pulled over and had a tap or two.

Now Glenn was quite a boxer from his days in the service, where he was one of the best, I guess. He said, "You boys get out and I'll show you some pointers about boxing." Earl Brown said, "I'm not much of a hand at boxing." But Glenn squared away with him anyhow and slapped him two or three times on the face. Very quick hands, you want to believe. Thing about Earl Brown, though, he was quick too, especially for a man of an awful size. He goes sideways and makes one lunge. He throws Glenn down and puts a foot on him. "That's the pointer I learned," he tells him.

But you can hear what you like about us getting into all kinds of fights; this, I believe, is mostly from people who never knew the real stories. About every fight was in good fun like the one I just spoke of, if they happened at all. Oh, a squabble over a card game maybe, but even then nothing to matter much. Folks was sweet-natured and had to be. You don't go on a river drive or anything else and work so hard and then have time or ambition for feuding with your own gang.

Spring of the year, I'd start in guiding, which was what I looked forward to. I did a lot of trapping in the bargain. We still set a few, Jack McElvey and I. One fall we caught twenty-seven mink, covered a lot of territory. You stand a better show to catch a mink in the little brooks than in one big river somewhere. I made a good scent; learned it from a gunsmithing man. And I have a very unusual shotgun myself, a .44. You can shoot a .44 bullet with it, but then you can buy fine shot to fit it too. Or you could once anyway. Some have often tried to buy that gun off me, but I still got her.

A gun's no way to end anything, and I know it; but you best turn your machine off, I suppose. I'm about talked out. For now, I mean.

Photograph by Steve Takach

Earl Bonness feeding a white perch to a loon on West Grand Lake.

Small Wonders

When I watched Sorn eating, I conjured a small but fierce animal. The boy hunched over the table, head low, arms encircling his plate, as if for fear that someone might try to steal his food. I had no doubt he'd snarl, lunge, bite if I reached a hand toward him. He looked cute as a button—and volatile as a cornered mink.

About two years later, when I introduced him to fishing on a Maine lake, I'd remember that earlier version of Sorn. The outing is nearly a decade past now, yet I can still feel the mesmeric rocking of my canoe among the waves of a July afternoon, can still picture the joy and mischief in his dark eyes.

We'd come to know the boy while my wife and I and three of the children—a son of sixteen, daughters of thirteen and nine—lived for half a year near Lugano, in Switzerland's only Italian-speaking canton, Ticino. For the spring semester I'd joined the faculty of a small American-administered college there with an international student body. That time in our careers was a delight, not least because of Sorn and his family.

My wife had met his adoptive mother at a luncheon put on by an expatriate women's group. The two had a first name in common. "Other Robin," or "Swiss Robin," as our family sometimes came to call her, was a comely American married to Giulio, a Ticino native. Their daughter Michelle matched up well in age and temperament with our youngest, my namesake daughter Sydney.

The two Robins soon met up again, having arranged a play date for Michelle and Sydney, who would go skating at a nearby rink. Europe being Europe, their mothers could chat over *cappuccini* at the rink's attractive café.

The girls circled the ice, and the two Robins soon recognized soulmates in one another. This led to our families' meeting for supper at Other Robin's home in the hamlet of San Antonino, forty kilometers north of our rented house near the college campus and the American academy that the two older kids attended. (Stalwart Sydney went to a nearby Montessori School, picking up Italian there by mere exposure, as children uncannily do.)

A visitor could hear three idioms in the Bognuda household: English, Italian and the local dialect, parts of which, when spoken slowly, I could understand. Its primary elements were evidently Italian but also included—along with some from Romansch, Ladino, and who-knows-what-else—a fair number from French. For instance, I recall the Antoninese word for *cherry,* perhaps because the fruit hung so copiously from one of their backyard trees. It's *cerese,* more like the French *cerise* than the Italian *cigliegie.*

Giulio proved charming, kind, and hilariously funny. His English was fluent, though unpolished, which contributed greatly to the comic effect. He told us that once he won Robin's heart years back, he gave up on learning her language grammatically; he could make himself perfectly clear on any subject, but couldn't grasp, say, the indefinite article: *a man* would always be *one man* to him, for instance, as in, "I was at work and one man told me this joke . . . "

Giulio also proved a fine cook, particularly at the hearth he'd wrought on their patio, complete with elegant stone chimney and a clever suspension device to lower or raise his grill as he chose. The Bognudas, like most Ticinesi, had a *grotto* too, a simple basement eating place, in which Giulio had installed a similar system.

I wonder whether his outdoor cooking paraphernalia represented European refinement as compared to our cruder American version at the Maine camp, a basic fireplace against which we prop archaic metal broilers. I could enjoy both methods almost equally, and it may have been no more than mere sentiment on my part—the recollection of so many family and friendly gatherings around our own blaze—that inclined me even slightly toward our more primitive approach.

As I say, however, the pleasures of that Swiss interlude owed a lot to the hours we spent by fires on the Bognudas' patio and in their *grotto*, and elsewhere in one another's company. We became close friends, and so, like them, if of course to a lesser degree, we anticipated with a mixture of apprehension, delight, and curiosity the Bognudas' trip to Thailand halfway through our sojourn. They'd be traveling to meet Sorn and, all being well, to bring him back from an orphanage in Bangkok.

Giulio, Robin and Michelle came to learn the boy was one of three hundred children at that facility, which had a staff of only four. No wonder the child protected his plate! Food had obviously been hard to come by in the years since his obscure birth. Sorn at four years old didn't weigh a lot more than a boy half his age; he was severely malnourished and had significant medical problems, chiefly respiratory, when he reached San Antonino.

And he had, in effect, no language, not even Thai.

Still, during the two weeks when his prospective parents and sister stayed with him in a Bangkok hotel, they all formed a sufficient bond for the new son to come home.

Home. I can't help but wonder what that concept may have meant to Sorn. He must have needed to learn it, as thoroughly as the languages he'd come to speak, but perhaps at greater effort.

After he'd been in Switzerland for a short time, however, I watched Sorn running, jumping, and somersaulting all over a certain lush meadow near the Bellinzona Castle, and I thought the whole while that I beheld a miracle even more wondrous than the emergence of some gorgeous butterfly from winter chrysalis. How quickly and improbably this energetic protégé had flown up and out of that swarmed orphanage!

From the start, of course, we would all now and then contemplate the fates of children who hadn't been so blessed, the parentless ones still there in Bangkok and indeed all over the globe, inarticulate, hungry, ill, and neglected, the ones who hadn't flown and might never. Yet here at least was this precious creature who'd rapidly transformed himself from feral guardian of his food to someone who could frolic like that—and could later savor, still avid but nonchalant now, one of Giulio's *risotti* or a chicken prepared by Swiss Robin or a simple sandwich, and do it all, yes, at home. You won't consider it sentimental if I tell you that Vermont Robin and I could get emotional over such a spectacle.

Two years later, in the summer of 2003, the Bognudas came to the States, as they do almost annually, to visit Robin's widowed father in Boston. We urged them to extend their stay and join us at the island camp, six or seven hours to the north.

They had less than a week to spend there, but happily, in a summer of pretty nasty weather otherwise all over upper New England, our days were fair ones. I found the evenings especially sweet, the kids playing board games in the cookhouse and the adults talking at fireside about what I can only and insufficiently describe as things that matter. Children and grandchildren, it seems, will bring that out in one man or one woman.

On the first night, hearing the boys and girls laughing and fussing inside over Boggle or Taboo, Vermont Robin recounted something, precisely, about games. Her story made me look foolish, as well it should have.

When our family was in Lugano, the two Sydneys would often play Blackjack, though we called it Pontoon, in the manner of my office mate, Christopher Matthews, a delightful Irish poet who became another fast friend.

My wife remembered that she'd often bring the female Sydney along when she crossed the border to take advantage of the cheaper Italian grocery prices. Opposite the market stood a toy store, where our daughter loved to buy Legos. Before too long, she'd amassed a major collection. Ingenious plastic constructions crowded the small living room.

Our Robin found it impressive that the girl had saved up so much of her paltry allowance and her birthday money. At length, however, she grew suspicious, and Sydney had to confess—or was it brag?—that she'd never once lost a game of Pontoon to me in our whole time abroad, and that each game had been played for stakes.

I have always found compulsive gambling beyond my ken. Still, exactly like some problem gambler, I clung to the notion that luck was simply bound to turn my way if I kept playing. As things developed, though, my luck remained steadily awful, and I must have lost as much as a hundred dollars in Swiss francs during the semester.

I laughed with the rest to hear Robin's tale, recalling how Sydney would look at me out of the corner of one slitted eye. "Pontoon?" she'd drawl like a gun moll, her lips barely parted, and down I'd sit at the dining room table, ripe for one more trouncing. I just didn't know how to play Pontoon, it appears. But there was a multitude of other things I didn't know during that Swiss sojourn, even if I can't be faulted for that. These are things I'd now pay a lot more than card money not to be obliged to know.

I couldn't, for instance, have forecast the catastrophe that would erupt on the 11th of September in that year, shortly after our return to Vermont. If someone had shown me photographs of people leaping out of enormous buildings, I'd have imagined Hollywood-style special effects. Nor, however crude his thinking had already proved, would I have guessed that a sitting president would launch the intemperate, illogical folly he called Iraqi Freedom in response to the Trade Center disaster, a war that killed scores of thousands to avenge three thousand American deaths.

Sitting there on our peaceable island, whenever I heard the distant drone of an airplane, I would discover myself brooding on the countless victims of conflict past and present. Would we ever learn? I'm afraid the realist in me said no, still does. There existed, and always will, enough suffering to go around on our gorgeous planet, but did that indelible misery make it more or less heartwarming for us all to see Sorn taking part in the other kids' entertainments?

I believe it made it more so. Those hours after supper seemed a reprise of that moment in the Swiss meadow, with Sorn cavorting carefree over its deep green. I'd think what I thought back then: in a world as cruel as this one can be, the salvation of a single small soul must be disproportionately meaningful. And their parts in such a redemption made mother Robin, father Giulio, and sister Michelle all the more precious as human beings.

Our little island struck me as a social paradise, however fragile and of course illusory, devoid not only of violence but also of the bigotry that so often engenders it. Shia and Sunni, Arab and Jew, Indian and Pakistani, Muslim and infidel, fundamentalist and agnostic, animist and janjaweed, Catholic and Protestant, black and white, gay and straight. The list seems endless.

The little Thai boy had already encountered milder forms of such prejudice at home, had experienced the thoughtless remarks and stares of adult and schoolmate alike. Narrow-minded, unconsidered opinions, of course, know no national boundaries, but the Swiss, even certain of the Latinate Ticinesi—so famous at once for prosperity and for xenophobia, one perhaps relating to the other—may have a better claim to that behavior than most.

Robin jokes that many Swiss view the Third World as beginning immediately on the far sides of their own borders. More seriously, Giulio recalls a neighbor's slur of an African woman who'd passed them in Lugano.

"*Putana!*" the neighbor muttered. Whore.

"How," Giulio marvels in disgust and disbelief, "can one man see one woman, only *see* her, and say this?" He shakes his head and breathes "*porco cane*," meaning literally "pig dog," but metaphorically commenting on the world's far-ranging idiocy.

But as I say, the world didn't seem in the least idiotic during the Bognudas' days with us at the camp. On the last of these, my friend Dave Tobey and I mounted our fishing trip. We headed for Fourth Machias Lake, which seemed a pretty safe bet. Once you locate a school of white perch there, it's generally a matter of cranking up one after another until you have enough for a fry.

Sorn sat on the thwart just ahead of me in the canoe's stern, Giulio in the bow; the pretty Robins, Sydney, and Michelle rode with Dave in a broad-beamed john boat he'd borrowed from his Uncle Junior.

I baited Sorn's hook with a night crawler and threw it over the side, showing him how to lower the worm until his line went slack, then reel it up a few turns to keep the bait off the bottom, away from the eels and hornpout.

There followed a very short interlude, during which I gazed at the tiny creature before me, backlit by a lazy blue sky, now and then briefly darkening as a cumulus ambled by overhead. A female merganser and her nearly grown clutch cruised at the mouth of Dead Stream in a long, long train; at my distance, I could have imagined some serpentine sea monster, but a friendly one.

I was startled from my reverie when Sorn's rod jerked savagely. Then the biggest smallmouth bass I'd seen in years leapt from the water. I watched the boy's mouth gape, his eyes widened to behold Behemoth right at their level.

He dropped the rod in his shock and alarm, but, fortunately enough, I was able to grab it just before the bass wrestled the whole rig over the gunwale. What had been a calm so deep, at least for me, that I could feel the tug of actual slumber became in the instant all high adventure, the brawny smallmouth towing my canoe from side to side at anchor, the fish's early runs so wild that I twice reached a hand to add a little heft to Sorn's rod, at which the boy—as he'd earlier done with his food—hunched, elbows out, and grimaced. Just as he'd warned against anyone's taking his supper two years before, he warned me now that the thing on that line was *his*, by God!

In time, and quite a bit of it at that, I managed to net the brute.

We released him, but not before we could snap a picture of Sorn holding up his bass by the lower lip. We still have the photograph of this handsome, copper-skinned boy and the bruiser, who stretches from the top of his head to his waist. The smallmouth looks to be about four pounds; Sorn can be little more than thirty. So our new angler's first fish turned out to be a creature weighing more than ten percent of what he did himself. I'd have had to tie into a bass of twenty pounds-plus to match him.

The bronze of the bass and Sorn's pigment were almost identical; his quivering echoed the subtle tremor of the fish, immobilized though it was by that pinch on the lip; the patina of the venerable canoe's hull planks shone under sunlight and blended with the mahogany of the wetland lake's surface. In short, the whole world in and around that slip of a watercraft seemed somehow lit both from within and without.

The poetry lover in me recalled the close of Elizabeth Bishop's stunning poem, "The Fish." Though the one she portrays is unlike Sorn's, having put up no fight at all, and though we were blessedly far from the pollutants Bishop mentions in her narrative, nonetheless the author could be describing the effects of our own scene, at least on me:

I stared and stared
and victory filled up
the little rented boat,
from the pool of bilge
where oil had spread a rainbow
around the rusted engine
to the bailer rusted orange,
the sun-cracked thwarts,

the oarlocks on their strings,
the gunnels—until everything
was rainbow, rainbow, rainbow!
And I let the fish go.

The universe was indeed as hopeful and auspicious as a rainbow, however momentarily. The smallmouth had arisen from the mysterious bottom layer of Fourth Lake, to which we returned it as quickly as we needed to. Sorn had arisen from a castaway's place in what was for us an exotic society; but he was not—no, never never never! —going to be put back.

Such, more or less, was my later reverie, from which I was called again, this time by my little fisherman's piping voice.

"Ooooh, Popcorns!" he cried, still quaking with adrenaline and delight at his catch. "Ooooh, *Popcorns!*"

I laughed aloud at the nickname, which Sorn had pinned on me back in Europe. He'd heard our daughter Catherine refer to me as Pops, and had misconstrued the word in a way that still delights me. Though Sorn's a young man of fourteen now, I hope I'll forever remain his Popcorns.

Addressed that way on Fourth Lake, I remembered the first time Sorn used the nickname. We were walking a cobbled street along the shores of Lake Lugano, the boy light as a leaf on my shoulders. As we passed some high roller's Ferrari Testa Rosa outside a restaurant, he cried, just as now, "Ooooh, Popcorns!" He'd come, in his short life as a Westerner, to love the mightiest automobiles he beheld; blending two of his languages, he called them "fortissimo cars."

So things had started wonderfully with our bass, and they stayed that way. Everyone—all the kids, Other Robin, Vermont Robin, and Giulio—caught fat perch after perch, Dave and I busy the whole while baiting and re-baiting hooks. A pair of loons, aroused by the action, came within a boat's length and circled, cackling and moaning for half an hour. At one point, Dave, sharp-eyed as ever, noticed an eagle perched above the Fifth Lake Stream ridge. One of our gang had just caught a young pickerel, and Dave twisted its neck and threw it about thirty feet. We all watched the mighty bird coast straight at us, as if trained to do so, dipping at last to snatch up the fish, then flying back to his lookout white pine.

The sun had begun lowering in the west, we had more than sufficient perch to cook in our big outdoor pan, and I didn't want to be cleaning fish in the dark. It had been a fine outing, all agreed. My one disappointment matched Giulio's. Whatever else he may have desired from his adventures in remote Maine, the most important thing was to see the animal he called *alce,* a word, needless to say, I hadn't needed in Italian. If I'd known the animal's Latin designation, *alces alces,* my friend would not have had to do his pantomime, hands cupped over his head to suggest palmated antlers.

Now if I'm not trying to show a visitor a moose, it seems, I practically have to shoo the big things out of the road. The moment I *want* them to appear, though, they might as well have gone extinct. So if it would be wrong to say we got into our trucks with heavy hearts, I for one did at least share some of Giulio's dissatisfaction at not having seen the *alce.*

When we took for home, however, I hadn't gone two hundred yards before a young bull trotted out onto the dirt logging road. Giulio was in Dave's truck behind me, so, after Sorn had had a good look, I pulled to the side to let the others pass. After Dave went by, our little caravan followed that animal as it cantered ahead for a quarter mile or so, before dropping a shoulder and clattering into a stand of alders.

The bull was far from full grown, his rack pretty modest by moose standards. But I'd almost bet our whole crew felt what I felt after the end of such a day.

Sometimes the small wonders are more than enough.

I looked down at Sorn, whose eyes were once again like saucers.

"*Fortissimo alce,*" I remarked.

"*Si,*" he answered, his face in an earnest frown. "*Si, Popcorns, fortissimo!*"

Daybook, August

I lay last night on the camp's dock and fell into a light sleep. When a baleful-sounding loon answered by another woke me, it was as though I'd suddenly discovered my own eyesight, and had never known its capacities before.

I gazed at the full moon, which lit up the shoreline, turning the mists along it into a great golden sash, seven or eight feet wide, which followed the island's contours. I almost believed I might walk the periphery to find that glowing band had enwrapped the whole mass like a Christmas ribbon.

But again I turned my gaze upward, trying to concentrate on a single star among millions—and failing. How could I not?

The poet Samuel Coleridge described awe as a condition in which you feel you are nothing. He felt that way in the great European cathedrals. I felt it just there where I reclined. I've felt so countless times. And yet such self-extinction seemed a balm.

Everything Comes Together

Late August, and cooler than it might be. Autumn impends, for which I will forevermore be a sucker, though I savor all the seasons.

This morning I mean to explore a little portion of local wildness I've never studied properly except in winter, when, frozen over, it can't show its true nature. I mean the swamp on the west side of our property, bordering the rock-strewn Old County Road, which was thrown up by the town about the time of my birth.

Why head to such a place? Because the day's itch has swamp in it. I can't explain myself better. Not yet. We shall see.

Even when the ice- and snow-cover let me pass over the swamp's real swampiness, I often feel some disquiet there. Not that the place holds anything truly dangerous; I won't fall into quicksand, the idea of which thrilled me to the spine during those childhood afternoons with their radio westerns. Peanut butter sandwich in one hand, root beer in the other, I'd shut my eyes and tip my chair against the Philco's blond cabinet listening to "Sky King," "The B-Bar-B Ranch," "Sergeant Preston," and such. I can still feel the throb of the speaker against my upper back.

No, there's no quicksand to make my gut clench, but like any swamp bigger than a quarter acre, this one does have its share of eeriness. Hard traveling too. I picture myself hopping from tussock to tussock, missing as often as I land, sinking to mid-shin or deeper.

As it turns out, despite late summer's plentiful rains, the swamp has all but drained itself. I can't make a bit of sense of that, and the surprise is oddly disappointing. Traveling to the far side proves so much quicker than I expected that I blink for a moment, as if adjusting my eyes to light after darkness, a darkness that wasn't there.

I'm suddenly and silently quoting from a poem. No, don't worry, I may be a poet, but I don't trip through wood and dell with verse dripping off my tongue. It's just that the passage that comes seems to fit this situation so exactly. And even better, the passage is one of the shamefully few I have by heart. Something called me to memorize it on my very first encounter.

You can find the lines in *The Prelude*, at a point where the young William Wordsworth gets excited, to say the least, by the prospect of finally crossing the Alps through the Simplon Pass. However, after he asks for directions from a peasant (who may well have thought of the local wonders as pretty much everyday stuff) our traveler discovers that he's already made his crossing!

Years later, in his reconstruction of the moment, Wordsworth says that, whether he knew it or not back then,

Imagination—here the Power so called
Through sad incompetence of human speech,
That awful Power rose from the mind's abyss
Like an unfathered vapor that enwraps,
At once, some lonely traveller. I was lost;
Halted without an effort to break through;
But to my conscious soul I now can say—
"I recognize thy glory" . . .

Now I don't want to overstate things here. To begin with, Wordsworth was traveling a well-worn path and I've been bushwhacking, following my nose and on the hunt for whatever rare openings in the under-story presented themselves. I've gotten where I am by choice, not, like Wordsworth, by mistake. I've sought improvisation, not stumbled into it. The distinction may seem petty, and in any case the real point is only that the great man and I revere imagination, as don't we all in some measure? For every person, however, no matter what he or she does or is, it's a matter of how that faculty gets stirred up.

If Wordsworth failed to find his "high" in nature, he could find it in mind. If my swamp's gone dry, let me hope my imaginative faculties have not. If I can use subverted expectations to produce a certain tang in experience, then even a disappointment doesn't have to disappoint.

And in fact, having missed the swampy quality of my swamp, I can still conjure or re-conjure other swampy episodes. Memory's a great aid to the imaginer—though it may also be an enemy, even direr than writing proves to anyone, bushwhacker or not, who dreams of witnessing things immediately as they occur. Not that either writing or memory lacks its benign aspects, as I hope I may have shown here and there in bumbling through these pages.

Just now it's precisely memory that takes me back sixty years, to cherished summer days when I'd accompany my Uncle Peter in a skiff up the Boquet River, on the New York side of Champlain. We went there after frogs, which we'd cook come evening over an open fire; I recall watching pale legs as they twitched galvanically in the pan. Soon we'd eat those small drumsticks. Uncle Peter was the only man on earth who actually laughed with a *yukyukyuk*. That million-dollar sound brightened the night, as it had the day.

I did all the shooting on those trips, with a .22 Remington scarcely longer than my forearm today. At my uncle's instruction, I aimed scatter-shot not at the prey but as close to it as possible, so the concussion stunned the poor frog but the meat went unharmed.

I'm sure I wouldn't take any child of mine to do what I so joyfully did on the Boquet. Times have changed—sensibilities too, my own along with the world's—and in our day there's the scary news that frogs are depopulating, the ones that endure frequently showing up deformed.

What lingers anyhow is much less the shooting than the oddly woolen smell of the bog and, more important, the way that smell can re-summon the affection I felt for my uncle. In these few years after his death at ninety-five, I may be inclined to talk about that feeling more elaborately than I could have a lifetime ago, when it was enough just to be in a certain place with a man who knew that place and what to do in it, and who seemed as fascinated by its life as the kid standing in front of him with a tiny rifle. Yes, today I may more directly address my love for that great soul, but real explanation, to echo my dear Wordsworth again, doth often lie too deep for tears.

In all honesty, another memory of the Boquet lingers too, even if this morning's ramble hasn't really jibed with it at all. I mean the recollection of swamp-dread, which descended upon the Adirondack evening as we reached the broad wetland at river's mouth. On the bank cross-stream, hard to see as the darkness lowered, we could make out the blackened remains of a shack, which had belonged to a woman named Evvie. It burned when I was seven, I think, its owner dying shortly afterward. I remembered nothing about Evvie except that she'd had a frightening face, which now would look more like a sad one, I'd bet.

But where did this memory come from? I asked my uncle about it years later, and he told me there'd been no such burn site, no such person. How, then, can I so clearly picture that place and even name that woman? Those images of things apparently nonexistent are as compelling and strange as today's swamp-that-is-no-swamp.

Does all this, as H. H. Munro once opined, derive from the fact that "the young have aspirations which never come to pass, the old have reminiscences of what never happened"? I can't make sense of that: the dread I felt in contemplating the charred house was never something I aspired to when young; nor is it something I reminisce upon for the sake of pleasure now.

Or maybe it is, though pleasure is surely an inexact term. It's perhaps rather that *image* is the root of *imagination*, and, as fellow Romantics have noted for centuries now, imagination can create realities as palpable as Chicago or Paris—or as Evvie's sad camp.

But how did I make the image of the blackened little building in the first place? I hadn't yet read any Hemingway in those days, hadn't read much at all besides the rotogravure Sunday comics that bled all over the kitchen table if I spilled my juice on them. Yet I'll claim, one's world moving strangely as it often does, that even if I obviously couldn't know it at the time, I was already looking ahead to "The Big Two-Hearted River," full itself of burned-over territory.

Nick Adams, Hemingway's protagonist, having fished all day in the upper reaches of the eponymous stream, decides not to enter the conifer-shadowed swamp he reaches just at dusk. He's afraid "the fishing would be tragic in the swamp."

My aborted scouting mission, along with the assorted memories it's kicking up, relates to Nick's situation and presentiment in the remotest way, of course, in part because, again, there's so little swamp in my own swamp this morning, and no tragedy whatever. Still I know what Nick meant, and I think—though who can be sure of such a matter?—I knew something about it a lifetime ago on the Boquet with my uncle, despite the fact that all those dear to me were alive and well, even our soon-to-be-gone cocker spaniel, Colonel. As far as I could see, God was in Heaven and all was right with the world.

My sense is that any longtime bushwhacker, rambler, and minor explorer would stand a good chance of catching Hemingway's drift too, because—no matter if the truly tragic is as absent from his or her life as from mine on that long-ago, unhurried stream—that person has found a swamp or two, and so gets it.

Gets what? What am I after here? Well, I suppose it's that I seem to care a lot less about what are called *ideas* in man, woman, landscape, or book than I care about indelible impressions like the one to which I've just referred, and I'm bold enough to suggest that the kindred spirits I've known share that inclination. And they may also find themselves struck by how, almost magically, one impression turns out to be a relative of all the others.

Not that I wish to dwell solely on somber impressions. Even if every word I write here sounds in some measure like elegy, I scarcely want melancholy to carry the day. I have left the swampless swamp, and above me now, near the height of a steep-sided ridge, my hearty pointer Pete has found something. I can hear as much. Or rather, the opposite: his collar bell just went silent; he's pointing.

It'll be a downright pleasure to see what that dog's up to, although he and I know the same thing today: it's not bird season yet, so he doesn't have to be anywhere near as single-minded as in a few weeks. No bird dog owns as much of that single-mindedness as a pointer. In October, Pete's sense of the target, to use boxers' parlance, makes even a flyweight look clumsy.

I marvel while I climb, just thinking about all that.

The whole way up the ledge-and-freestone slope is make-it-as-you-can, hands, knees, elbows, feet, and I keep telling myself I used to do this sort of thing more easily and vigorously. But my wife reminds me I've sung that tune all the decades she's known me. She claims it's why I'm such a sap for Wordsworth, who was already worried about physical and mental decline at twenty-eight!

Wife's opinion or no, in my older age I have to pause now and then on this steepness, and while I do, I think about dead Belle, another of my gun dogs. Once, out of season too, she stopped and pointed into a blank clear-cut some quarter mile east of me here. She just wouldn't move. She kept holding that point, mind you, over old snow just crusting.

She stood there, locked up, statuesque as a dog in some plutocrat's oil painting from a bygone quail-shooting era. I could yank her away, or I could walk past her and learn what turned out to be what, which I assumed would be nothing. Then, assuming nothing, I was embarrassed, even if no one but the dog herself was there to witness, as a sure-to-God something exploded out of that blankness. A grouse had been hiding under the snow, hoping it wouldn't ice up entirely and lock him in, but planning to stay as long as he could before showing himself to us.

In one of the great Raymond Chandler's novels, some punk warns Philip Marlowe that he could make the detective need some new bridgework. Marlowe replies, "You could also play centerfield for the Yankees and hit a home run with a breadstick." Belle's point was that improbable. Another day, another quotation in the wild.

I could recite other jaw-dropping examples of their behavior as I call to mind all the good dogs I've been lucky enough to be with in woods or by water. But just now, on this ridge, I discover this particular one—and never mind his blue blood—digging like a terrier for a chipmunk. Or maybe, delusional, he imagines that the red squirrel scolding him from the lightning-halved white pine behind us is not up there at all but only a few inches deeper into the ground, just under the bottom of the crater he's carving.

Whatever the case, I'm disproportionately amused, even overjoyed. Both of us are on a holiday, and not.

I'm really talking about more than random impressions, you see. I want to get at the notion that everything comes together. It's a sort of woodsman's version of faith—or one woodsman's anyway. It's a sense of the shapeliness of things in the aggregate: the good and bad; the predictable and surprising; the phantom red squirrel or chipmunk of my pointer's fancy; the murky vision of travel through murky wetland; frog and grouse; ridge and dry swamp; today and decades ago; a screwdriver-sized .22 Remington and a burnt-over cabin.

It all comes together. It must.

Why should this theme of inclusiveness fall on me in certain places, even or especially in unlikely ones like this? Who knows? There's no landmark to provoke it here, that's for certain; there's only that storm-punished pine, otherwise hardly different from hundreds of others on this hill, and that mound of earth flung up by a silly gun dog.

Nothing, it seems, should inspire this grandiosity. I haven't crossed any Simplon Pass, nor failed to. For all of that, though I may be inexcusably vain to say so, this morning the jolt of recognition Wordsworth experienced in Switzerland—the zing of Imagination's "awful power"—seems available to me, a simple low-mountain prospector, as it has on many and many a hike.

In imagination, anything can live next to anything else.

Fall

Daybook, Late September

There was no reason for it, but I woke up yesterday with that copper penny taste on my tongue, purple brackets at vision's edge, legs unwilling to swing from bed—all the familiar signs of dejection.

To force myself outside and into the northwester was instant cure. I smelled someone's woodsmoke as it raced by me on the blow, and a whiff of bacon from an open kitchen window. Or maybe not from a window. Maybe that someone was cooking breakfast on an outdoor fire, despite the weather. I didn't get within fifteen feet of the river, but I felt its spray on my face, the cleanest, dearest water I'll ever know.

Perhaps it was the wild and scattered day that made my thoughts blow around too, as if on the northerly wind that roared down from the lake to checker the flow above my camp. The waves on the lake itself must have been taller than I am.

At any rate, as so often, back inside I started thinking of Earl Bonness on a day like this. It was only middle summer, but the wind seemed to blow a taste of autumn our way. The two of us sat and talked for hours, because, in his words, "There's no doin's on the water today." We kept reminiscing about gone friends, including my father. Earl punctuated our recollections by repeating, almost like a chant, "Men we've known, Syd. Men we've known."

Somehow I remembered walking outside to pee at one point, the two of us having drained a full pot of coffee. On the way back, I bent and plucked an unripe blueberry from a bush by the river. The gloss-green skin resisted my bite, but then came a sudden burst of tartness, which struck me as improbably perfect. I looked for one just like it yesterday morning, but of course the year's berries were long gone.

As I went back indoors that morning, the screen door flapped. I forced it shut and latched it. The downriver corner where Earl sat was dim. I blinked my eyes a few times, adjusting the gloom until it wasn't gloom.

For some reason I told Earl about Freddie Dunbar, who'd lately been killed back home as he walked along Route 10 at midnight, the poor fool, treading that road in the same black overcoat he wore in heat and cold alike. He held no light in his hand. I suspect he didn't own one.

Freddie was one walking man. He often passed our house, headed for the old cellar hole on Skunk Hollow Road, where his family's house had stood a generation back, before it burned. I'd hear his incantation—*Mama, Mama, Mama*—full of terrible sadness at her death, at the loss of the home place.

He was that anachronism, the village idiot, his speech always garbled, his look confused, but he was sweet-natured, harmless. His mission in life consisted of hiking from one town fair to another, July to Labor Day, sometimes as far as Newport, eighty miles north. He must simply have liked to behold those fairs in all their tinsel glory. He can't ever have had money for a ride or cotton candy or girlie tent.

He went, he came back.

Earl remembered his own town's village idiot, though I've forgotten his name by now. He'd died before my time here. Such people were merely taken for granted in the region. New England towns had Overseers of the Poor until not so long ago, and folks like Freddie got a pittance to spend, a local family a pittance to board them. So the death of Freddie marked the death of one more aspect—to be wondered at rather than sentimentalized—of the old-time north country.

"Men we've known," Earl repeated, "men we've known." But he also cautioned, "You can't live in the past." I wonder if he meant that the effort to do so, which I've often over-indulged, was a sort of suicide. Did Earl mean that striving to sustain oneself on reminiscence alone would literally starve him to death?

I'm not sure. But I mean to take it that way just now. I mean to make Earl and all the revered elders a part of today, to feel them in this overbearing wind, with all its odors and other sensations, which has blown me back to my senses. I'm not sure what I mean by saying that's what I mean to do, but I do mean it. Whatever it means.

Turned Around

Such hours as I'd spent in the neighborhood of West Grand Lake by the time I was twenty were almost exclusively on the water. I hadn't yet learned much of the countryside surrounding the lakes. But I had an itch to go deer hunting over the 1963 Thanksgiving break, and—my long love affair with that territory and its citizenry already well launched— I could think of no better ground for the hunt.

It seems odd that I remember nothing about how I ducked the obligation to go home for the holiday. My mother could be given to melodrama, or, more effective, to demonstrative, guilt-inducing resignation: sighs, frowns, slumped shoulders. It would not surprise me, though, if my father, more forbearing and more woodsy, had approved my plan and even lobbied for it.

Be all that as it may, on Tuesday evening, after a meal in Topsfield, I settled into my room at Weatherby's Lodge. Before sleep, however, I studied a topographical map, having passed the afternoon of my first day hunting woods along the Big Lake Road, close to the village, with complete disbelief in my prospects. Things just didn't feel right. I concluded that tomorrow would change for the brighter; I'd be up on Little River Mountain.

The choice was arbitrary. I'd never been on that hill, though I'd canoed several miles downstream from it on Little River itself, jump-shooting ducks with one of my life's great mentors, Creston MacArthur. So I couldn't have told you why its very name drew me like a magnet, except that there had already been times in my past when some unaccountable hunch ended up being on the money.

Fish the heavier water today, I told myself at some point, for example, and came home with a creel's worth of trout.

Hunt that patch of cedar, I thought some other time, and for no logical reason those woods held one grouse shy of a limit.

When in doubt, I believed, count on inspiration.

I got up and out the next morning before the kitchen crew arrived, and, nothing if not eager and reckless in those days, without telling anyone where I was headed. I just stuck the ham sandwich I'd made the night before into a pocket of my mackinaw, loaded my gun and pack into my dinged-up Volkswagen Beetle, and took off southwest from town.

Five miles out, I parked and followed a northerly trail, which the map said would lead me to the mountain. That landmark was no more than a knoll, really, some seven hundred feet high, but that's an eminence in such flat country. Trusty inspiration had indicated I'd find good deer sign on her south-facing slope.

In fact, I ran into considerable sign well before I got that far. The snow lay patchy, just ten to forty square feet here and there, interrupted by equal expanses of bare ground. But even the bare spots were wet enough to keep a track. I followed a big one west, off-trail, dreaming a monster buck the whole while. After a spell, though, I came to a maze of beaver-work and lost it.

I never would become much good at following sign, deer hunting always a lesser passion for me than birds over a pointing dog, and I had even smaller skill then. I'd be no Dave Tobey, no Joey Olsen. The deer I shot as a younger boy had all lived in Pennsylvania farm country; you could set up at field's edge or near an orchard and reasonably expect an open shot if you'd done a little scouting. But I was after deep-woods prey that morning, not the grain-fed, pastoral variety.

Back at the trail, I shocked myself on consulting my watch: I'd lost not only that impressive set of tracks but also nearly an hour and a half. It was already 8:30. I still had all day, of course, no one waiting for me. I hadn't chosen a meal plan at Weatherby's; it'd be cheaper to drive up Route 1 to Chick Daggett's store for my suppers.

But the money wasn't primary. I liked the *scene* at Chick's, the hub of tiny Topsfield, Maine. You could cut the stove-and-cigarette smoke in that lunchroom with your scabbard knife—a different era. Loggers and hunters gathered at all times of day, full of boasts and stories, a fair number true; and Chick had a way of hiring the best-looking young women in the county to work in his place. There were plenty of reasons, in short, to pass some time in his establishment.

Maine didn't yet have the moose lottery that it does today, but the menu always included a "Mooseburger Special." I ordered it every time, assuming I'd be eating a Canadian animal or a poached one. I now suspect that Chick had come up with the whole business for local color, that what I chose, dinner after dinner, was in fact just cheap ground beef. No matter, I savored each chewy bite.

Chick's smacked of old-time upper New England in every way. You didn't introduce yourself to anyone; you showed up often enough, as I'd done in a couple of fishing seasons, signed a check or two, and in due course the regulars would start to call you by name. They did, that is, once you proved yourself worthy of such personal address, which meant indicating some knowledge of game, of woods and waters, of hunting and fishing, though you had to do so in a way that didn't make you look like a braggart. That was pretty easy for me. I didn't have a hell of a lot to brag about.

A relative beginner like me did better, anyhow, to say less than he listened. I particularly recall one man to whom all the others deferred; they called him Tippy, a strangely cute diminutive. Tippy's deer-hunting theory was simple: a good buck bedded on the opposite side of the ridge he fed on. You could intercept your deer on that line if you could make out how it ran.

I'm not at all sure this gospel had any merit at all; I never could prove it myself, and I tried, believe me. Yet Tippy, it appeared, was a legendary local deer-slayer. And all these years later, I do believe in his theory in a way. That is, I think a hunter or angler inevitably develops personal superstitions, and if he believes in them sincerely enough, they'll work out. Confidence has as much to do with outdoor success as anything.

I would later meet another mentor, a gruff Vermonter named Ray. He wouldn't even bother to fish the Batten Kill for brown trout if the barometer was headed downward. No point, he claimed. Even back then, I suspected that his dogma might be overblown, yet how could I challenge a man who, having implicit trust in it, killed eye-popping fish each time he waded that notoriously challenging stream?

Ray, you will say, would have done the same under the conditions he deplored, given his endowments. But perhaps not. No matter his undeniable skills both with a fly rod and at the tying vice, the man's near-religious faith constantly reassured him; lacking it, he might not have been so productive.

But now I've gotten as far off my story's trail as off that other trail, the one I stood on in a morning nearly fifty years ago. My point is that I hoped the dream of Little River Mountain would prove my own mystical secret to success.

The day had started fair as fair could be. When I set out, I beheld stars in their millions through my windshield, each sharp as a dagger against the darkness. By true dawn, however, about seven o'clock, the wind turned and flew out of the east, cloud cover drifting in from the ocean forty miles distant. I remember thinking, At least it's not right at my back. I still had a notion that once the mountain materialized, I'd be climbing its southern flank, studying fresh buck sign, and I didn't want to be upwind when that happened.

As things developed, my arrival there would again be interrupted. I came upon a heel-heavy track that crossed a patch of snow on the trail, auspiciously moving into the wind. I began another stalk to eastward, but before long I lost that track too. The animal had swung through a thick growth of softwood, and I didn't own enough savvy, the snow so spotty under the trees, to stay with it over the acre or two of needle spills.

I say it wasn't long before I lost that track, but in fact I surprised myself once more. It seemed I'd spent the better part of an hour creeping after the buck—if buck it was, I'll never know. By now it was 10:30, and I could scarcely calculate for sure how far uptrail I'd come. The map's scale showed the mountain at about two miles from where I'd parked the car, but, preoccupied, I hadn't been thinking about such a matter at all.

Of course, I'd been moving along slowly, more slowly than I eventually learned to do when not amid fresh evidence of deer traffic. Yet at last I began to see contours of the mountain through gaps in the trees. This slowed me even further, as if on gaining a full view of that hill I'd behold a ten-point whitetail, broadside in open woods.

Some few hundred yards shy, I encountered a real obstacle: the wind had at some point swept together a great tangle of blowdown, which lay across the trail and extended fifty yards to the standing woods on either side. A line gale, I figured, had whipped off the big lake a mile or so to my right. I cut in that direction, hoping to skirt the whole mess, but I fetched up again at a beaver bog. To wade it would take me over my boot-tops. So I turned the other way, managing at length a half-moon scramble around the west end of the tangle and back to the footpath.

This also took longer than I figured it might, but now at least the rise before me showed plainly. The woods on the sidehill, however, proved anything but open; they showed evergreen growth for the most part, and I saw no clear trail up. Making my way through the density, I grew more and more careful about where I put my feet, more and more attentive to any hint of game.

I remember flushing a grouse from behind a rootball; I hadn't expected that explosion, and it about scared me silly. Once I settled, however, I began to discern scrapes and cuffings, the latter pretty fresh, not a single frost crystal yet in the riled earth; and after a matter of twenty yards, just that much higher from where I'd been treading, the track of a deer showed plain in the snow. A large deer.

Carter White had told me that a hoof held about the same degree of body heat as a human hand. You could put your hand into the snow next to a track and time how long it took for the snow to melt to the same depth. That would tell you more or less how long it had been since the animal passed.

The idea made no sense and still doesn't. A hoof-print is made by weight, not temperature. Could this have been another of those self-generated hunter's tenets? Or was it merely a practical joke? Carter surely had that in him. In the instant, I recalled a farmer who, when I was about thirteen, assured me that my mustache would grow out like a man's within a week if I smeared hen manure on my lip before bed every night. I won't go further into that, still a bit embarrassed a lifetime after.

But I didn't worry long about the possible likeness of Carter's advice to that damned farmer's; anything Carter said inclined me to belief. He was a god in my estimation. I came up with a rough count of six minutes. My fingertips burned with the cold by the time I pulled my hand back—but six minutes were only six minutes.

The deer's trail meandered. He seemed in no hurry. I saw a place or two where he'd stood on his hind legs to crop a hanging hardwood tip, others where he'd paused to leave his dark urine, tinged with a hue almost red from glandular secretions. My heart started to talk to me.

The wind still came east, and I made sure to stay downwind of the whitetail's trail. I didn't know enough then, and never really would, to "pattern" him, but I hoped I knew how to keep that breeze above me.

The hanging clouds now began to spit a nasty something between rain and snow, but not heavily enough to cover what I followed. I was mainly impressed by how the change in weather *darkened* everything. Inside the heavier thickets, it felt like night.

By now my watch said one o'clock. How did that happen so quickly? In such a far northern place, at this time of year the sun would be setting by four. Again I tried to reckon how long it would take me to walk back to the VW, but I'd made so many detours, and that big blowdown had so delayed me, I still had no basis for figuring. And I hadn't brought a compass with me, a choice I'd made out of some absurd inkling that to carry such a device might take the edge off the kind of direct, unmediated outdoor experience I pursued, even then, almost as passionately as I ever have pursued my quarry. I'd never seen Carter consult a compass, and for some reason it didn't occur to me that that was because he'd trod this country for sixty years.

No one knew where I stood at that moment, my family seven hundred miles away, people at the lodge not expecting me for the evening meal. It made sense to leave this critter for tomorrow, Thanksgiving Day, but sense hardly prevailed in my make-up back then.

At eighteen, a man doesn't believe he'll ever die anyhow, really. Hell, I figured, I may not have a compass or even a light, but if worse comes to worst, I do have a sweater in my pack, along with a waterproof canister of matches and a poncho. And hadn't Carter once told me that a man didn't have all the experience he'd need in life if he hadn't spent at least one unplanned night in the woods?

At last I swore I saw the twitch of a tail-flag, but, having inched along, eyes up and fixed, I found a young beech still clinging to its summer's leaves, which shimmied in the breeze. The encroaching blackness was playing loose with my vision. Yes, I needed to turn for the road after all. A little after three now; I had to move right along. I wouldn't see much of anything in an hour.

When I came to that conflicted sprawl of blown-over wood, I knew which way to go to get around it. I could make out my own tracks from some hours past, if just barely, or rather my hands-and-knees scrapings.

I remembered how the footpath broadened just past the snarl. If I could reach it soon, I'd have time to beat full darkness, fit and young as I was.

Yet now my heart began to thump again, this time with a tinge of ominousness. These dog-hair woods were no place to be caught once the light failed. I understood as much with all that heart just now.

I'd been taught by my father and others that the worst thing I could do in a tight situation outdoors was to panic. But something very like panic was taking charge as I went down on hands and knees to slither under that wall of brush and timber. In doing so, worse luck, I managed to scrape my glasses off.

It had darkened so, especially under that pile, that I couldn't even spot the glasses' gold frames and bright lenses among the rotted sticks and needles. I stayed in one place, still in a crawling posture, and groped on the ground with ungloved hands. Every few seconds, I believed I felt glass or metal. But with every shot of hope came the quick and sobering recognition that I'd merely latched onto a cold twig.

I wasn't even sure I'd be able to see my wristwatch if I looked at it now; I scrupulously avoided that, however, fearful of what I might find on the dial. Still I knew I simply couldn't wait any longer. I rose and blundered back toward the trail, or where I believed it lay.

My eyesight weakened, I must have crossed that trail unaware. After a few minutes, convinced this was exactly what I'd done, I walked one way and then the other, making myself move deliberately, scanning what little I could of the ground for the way out.

None of the old woodsmen I've known ever told me they'd been lost. They admitted only to being "turned around." That seemed euphemistic but accurate for my situation. I couldn't really be certain anymore which direction was which, though I'd have hiked to the road easily enough had daylight lasted.

Which it hadn't. So I decided just to follow my gut idea of south, to walk a direct line in that direction even if this meant crashing through all but impenetrable brush whenever I ran into it, which was plenty. The straightness of my progress would be essential; I didn't want to wander around like an ampersand. I hoped at length to come out somewhere on the Little River Road. Then, half blind or not, I'd follow it east or west, eventually finding my car in one of those directions and heading home, squinting over the dashboard to keep to the rough track.

Home: it seemed my heart's desire in that hour, though for a year and some, home had been no more than my messy room in a dormitory—a room that nonetheless glowed in my mind now.

I began to wish for a moon, that flat-topped one of late fall, perhaps not enough to light my way but enough to prove it the *right* way. I knew no moon would be showing so early, though, nor would it later—not through that cold mizzle.

I just kept walking, abraded at every step by branches, stumbling and more than once falling into a pothole or tripping over rock or root. I could have struck a match to check the time, but I didn't want to waste one of the too few I'd brought. And I still didn't want to know how late it had gotten, or how early, depending on the perspective I chose. The hours I might be spending alone out there would no doubt pass as slowly as my grammar school detentions, which I'd endured in abundance. Why not? I was a bad kid, and was being punished even now.

I may have staggered along for half an hour before I acknowledged that my stay would indeed be an extended one. Feeling with my feet for a level plot, I took the pack from my shoulders, lit one of those matches after all. There remained some luck in the world; I was in the midst of a clump of cedar, dense enough for shelter, and each lower branch dead and dry enough for a blaze.

I took my knife from its sheath and, fumbling a bit in the dark, cut a fringe of shavings along one of the sticks, as my father had shown me to do in those school days. I covered the frayed stick with a witch's hat of twigs and touched it off. The fire kindled with gratifying speed, and before long, using thicker and thicker pieces to feed the flame, I had something that would do me.

By the firelight I saw a fair amount of downed deadwood, and I made it my business to fetch every last bit I could right away, making a substantial stack close by. I'd be free from the chill at least for a while. Mercifully, the frozen stuff had stopped pipping on the canopy. Things seemed to be going my way, at least compared to how they might have.

Maybe some hunter driving in late from farther out of town would see my rig, I dreamed, and lean on his horn to guide me out. Or maybe the folks at Weatherby's would after all notice I hadn't returned, no light showing in my rented cabin. I knew this was a faint hope: I'd made a point the night before of staying at Chick's for at least an hour after supper, listening to the talk, drinking endless cups of coffee, my bladder and my sleep unchallenged by caffeine and liquids at so young an age.

Chick's didn't close till 8:00, and the drive back to the village from there took all of forty minutes. By the time I got in that first night, Alice and Bev Weatherby and all their staff had been in bed an hour, and would be again tonight, needing to get up before dawn to accommodate their other hunters. Come morning, they might send someone looking—and they might not: I didn't eat any breakfast at the lodge either, or anywhere else.

From right then until whenever the Weatherbys noticed my absence— perhaps after a chambermaid reported my unmussed bed—would feel like an eon. But with any good fortune I'd be on my way out come false dawn anyhow, using the pale eastern sky, no matter the overcast, in place of the moon, or the damned compass I should have carried.

I knew enough, at least rationally, not to worry about wild things. The bears were all asleep by now, and none had ever killed anyone in New England anyhow that I'd heard tell. We didn't have coyotes in those days, but they're no threat either, at least not to humans, now that we do.

If I had small reason to fear the wildlife, however, in this circumstance reason scarcely ruled the game. Something would shuffle dead leaves close by, and the roots of my hair would tingle. At one point an owl's eight-note report from a limb just above seemed the hooting of the Devil himself as he broadcast my sins to the world. I needed more than a few minutes to calm after hearing that yammer.

Looking back, I see that even at that age my life was as much literary as anything else. Someone—I wish I could remember who—has since described me as "a man in the woods with his head full of books, and a man in books with his head full of the woods." Sitting by my glowing coals, small drops from the boughs above me now and then plummeting into them with a modest hiss, I began to imagine myself as the unnamed man in Jack London's famous "To Build a Fire."

I had no dog, of course, to contemplate murdering, as I wouldn't have had to do in any case. It was about 38 degrees where I sat, as opposed to negative 75; my wilderness was a pretty small one compared to London's Yukon; and even if those droplets were to douse my fire, as they would not, I'd find myself in no danger of freezing.

And yet, having read "To Build a Fire" as a freshman in high school, I discovered I could import the sense of doom that the story had so vividly evoked. There seemed a sort of tonic excitement in that literary allusion, though under my shiver and despair lay my wiser self, which mocked such bookishness; that wiser part of me was subtle enough as barely to be perceptible, but at length it sufficed to bring me back to my actual circumstance—which soon became an exquisite tedium. There I lay, my shoulders against a soft, rotted stub, stirring only to flop another piece of tinder onto the fire, which endured beyond my expectations.

But that success proved slight comfort at best. Thinking back on the indescribable creeping by of those hours, I imagine a long jail sentence. How can some felon bear the time bearing down? He can read, I suppose, a recourse that so often gets me through an otherwise idle span, and whatever the circumstance, frequently feels transportative. But to our inmate, mere literature, whether refined or common, must seem so artificial and ultimately so non-redemptive that it simply melds with his boredom. Of course I didn't have a book in any case. Why in hell would I? I had no more than my thoughts.

I don't know how often I lapsed into sleep or half-sleep, nor, when I did, for how long. I'd bet, however, those respites were far briefer than the periods of wakefulness. During the first few of those, already a man of words, or rather a boy, I tried to recite such poetry as I knew by heart. I was dismayed by how little that amounted to. Worse than knowing none, I halfway knew a lot, and the frustration of having three of four stanzas, say, or *almost* all the words of a concluding couplet, proved food itself for insomnia. I gave up after four or five efforts.

But my mind soon went in other unhelpful directions, whose sole virtue lay in disrupting the dullness. My father, for example, was an unusually good man, and in my better self I knew it.

I remembered my mother telling him, "The trouble with you is that you're a damned saint!"

"It won't hold up in court," he replied.

If I never saw my dad again, would I be satisfied that I'd shown him due affection, even reverence? As it turned out three years later, the answer was no, but I could hardly predict as much in '63.

What about Mr. Roller, that teacher my peers and I so abused in sixth grade that he had a nervous breakdown? Where might he be now? Too late, I wished him well and meant it.

And what about my most recent girlfriend? At the end of the preceding summer, I'd broken up with her. Like so many young romances, ours didn't prove stout enough against protracted absence. Margot's college was in New York State, mine in Connecticut.

I remembered part of the letter she sent me: "With you I was only a satallite." *Satallite*? Good Lord. Good riddance. Anyhow, by now I'd started wooing Ginny, a student at another institution. (My own had not yet gone coeducational.) She could claim, at the very least, to be my intellectual equal.

I pointedly corrected my ex's misspelling of *satellite* in a brief and snide return note. It didn't occur to me, though, to contemplate her charge that I'd somehow dominated the relationship. Or rather I did consider and dismiss it. I took the misspelling to suggest, as I made clear, that my efforts at instructing her had failed. She'd do well, then, to look for someone more on her own level.

Mean-spirited as my letter did intend to be, I hope with all my heart I didn't put matters quite so savagely, not to mention pretentiously, but I know such was the gist of the thing, and I wince at all this today, though I didn't in those woods.

Or I didn't at first. That hard mix started to fall from the black sky again, rattling my tenuous cover of boughs, and I thought perhaps I'd been dead wrong not to try winning back Margot's affections. Time passing, I more and more remembered her as the lovely and decent girl she was. What on earth had I done—or not done? I could see her pretty smile in the shimmering coals at my feet, could recall a magic night at the old Sunnybrook Ballroom, where one of the big bands—all crumbling by then in the new rock 'n' roll era—played songs from my parents' generation. The fire's warmth on my face brought to mind her cheek, warm on mine as we danced to the slower numbers.

Goddamn, I thought, *I'm lonely.*

At least gloom had replaced the boredom. I now began to think that the apparent receptiveness of my new love interest at Smith College was actually mere politeness. I wouldn't win her affections, or anyone else's. Now I rued the rancorous split from Margot, falling more deeply in love with her by my campfire than I'd ever been when we were together. Without her, I was certain, I couldn't live.

Of course I've lived for ages since. Back then, though, as I'd never done before, I studied some of the profundities involved, precisely, in living: the meanings of existence, of death, of love, of my each and every action, which struck me now as deeply misguided, even immoral— enough so to land me in this fix.

I'd never get out.

Not that I was back in Jack London territory. I didn't mean I'd physically perish in these slushy woods. I was thinking in a more metaphorical way, a tendency that has been both blessing and curse ever since. I supposed, instead, that I'd come to a permanent spiritual place, utter solitude its defining feature.

Once again, some saner part of my brain must have scoffed at such melodrama even as fancy played it out. Still I did wonder if Carter's claim, that a man needed at least one lost night outdoors to know what he had to know, signified something far different from what I'd inferred. I assumed the old man was talking about a lesson in resourceful woodcraft, but he may have meant something about facing up to the grander issues. Of which I saw that I knew nothing. I only knew that I was companionless, my literal solitude nothing compared to my permanent mental one.

Did that one night crack open a door, however slightly, to a metaphorical path (there I go again) toward something exactly opposite, away from nihilism and, at least in time, toward a greater engagement with those I cared about, especially wife and blood kin, but also friends and even strangers?

I could say so, but I'd mistrust, as ever, my capacity to make coherent narrative of jumbled experience. If I've turned out to be a teller of stories, on the page and otherwise, old-fashioned ones with beginning, middle, and end, down in my soul I still know that life doesn't proceed in so orderly a fashion. I know, in other words, that my instinct to the verbal, nearly catastrophic at times, may actually be my substitute for a coherent vision of life, not the vision itself.

And yet again, it's the dream of coherence that keeps me from the nihilist's despair.

Round and round I go.

No, I'm not sure whether or not that dark sojourn near Little River Mountain had a thing to do with my later opinions and feelings, baffled and illogical as these would sometimes become in later life. It had taken me half the night and more to consider anything at all besides my own comfort—the fire, the poncho, the ham sandwich, which at last I remembered and devoured—and my plan, if I could call it so, to escape this fastness at earliest light.

As it happened, I didn't have to wait that long. I'd just flopped another piece of wood on my fire, and seen, as the log caught, that it was two in the morning, when I heard the far rumble of an engine, faint at first, but growing less so by the moment.

By God, that was a log truck!

The driver must have been hauling a late—or maybe an early—load from somewhere to my west along the Little River Road. Even back then, the paper companies were at it twenty-four hours a day. I traced the sound's progress for a minute, and it told me exactly how the road lay. I likely stood no more than two hundred yards from it! My sense of direction had not been far off; I must have walked fewer than fifteen degrees east of south those hours before.

I crashed out to the road before the truck could reach me there. The driver slowed. He didn't stop. Rifle in one hand, I hopped onto his running board and held on as best I could with the other to his wing mirror. When the man rolled down his window, I asked if he'd seen my car, his big rig still rolling as I spoke.

Short and wiry, he looked at me inquisitively at first, then muttered something I scarcely heard. I knew in the instant he was a French speaker, perhaps over from the St. John valley. His *joile* dialect confounded me, but he could understand me when I repeated the question in schoolboy French.

Vous avez remarqué ma voiture?

He smiled, then jerked his thumb behind him. My wheels lay that way.

Merci beaucoup! I whooped, hopping off.

In a quarter mile I came on the trail-worn Beetle.

I decided I'd return for an hour or so of sleep at the lodge, drive to Topsfield for breakfast, then head back to the Little River Mountain trail by ten, my buck still out there, at least in my imagination.

It was Thanksgiving, but I still figured Chick's would be open. I could buy a compass there.

Carter White, legendary guide, deerslayer, trapper, and guide.

Refurbishment

I'm all geared up to go after grouse with my local Maine pal Dave. In the dooryard, my truck has idled a minute, its windshield defrosting. Seven a.m. Time to head out, but before I do, I glance at the mirror over the rough pine dresser given me by Creston MacArthur more than forty years back.

Is it something about the mirror itself, full of ripples and scratches, or perhaps that the damned thing hangs just here, in the river camp my ex-brother-in-law and I bought for a song all this lifetime ago? *A lot of water over the dam.* The platitude seems irresistible. I hear the river rushing over Big Falls, and when I turn, I see a small salmon leap, as if in simple exuberance. A flash and gone. A lot of water indeed, and my own leaping days well gone too.

This place had stood abandoned for years. Fishing the river from foot to mouth, as I did almost every summer's day as a very young man, I'd notice the little structure, built in the neighborhood manner: half-round logs on the vertical for siding. Working alone, a man would have found it harder to keep those timbers on the horizontal as he placed them. I'd later learn that Red Yates put the cabin up in the '30s. Today I can imagine him, however accurately. Autumn looming, he braces a log with a fore-arm and a knee, hammering eight-penny spikes with the free hand, the nose of a vanilla flask peeking out his back pocket.

Red and his wife raised a family in this tiny shelter, which stood a hundred yards east, up on the Big Lake road. Then, in the middle '50s, a doctor from upstate New York bought it and hired a crew to move the whole show to river's edge.

131

Sadly, the doctor's wife soon lapsed into mental illness, often severe enough to require institutionalization. Her husband, preoccupied with this harrowing course of events, rarely found time to visit his Maine camp. He mailed a check to Paul Hoar, the savvy owner of the general store, to see to its boarding up.

That poor woman. That poor doctor. They were probably not yet forty. A slew of years stretched ahead, too many of them blighted. So I muse just now. I didn't have many such thoughts whenever I passed their Big Falls cabin in those days. As I say, I did occasionally glance at it, but I don't remember pondering—at least not for some spell—how wonderful a place it would be to own. This indifference might have seemed strange to a tourist even then (how many have commented on my good fortune since?), but as a youngster utterly intent on fish, I was hard to distract, and disinclined to think past the day in which I found myself.

Standing by the falls, I'd be looking for a rise above them, or else swinging a streamer or bouncing a nymph below. The camp yard was no more than a space to cross on my way up- or downriver. No salmon swam through the ledge or the rough grass, after all. And my parents had a camp uplake on an island. What did I need?

In those days, my brother-in-law and college classmate was an aide to Governor Ken Curtis, and he was looking for a spot, not impossibly far from where he lived in Wiscasset, to wet a line for wild fish. He and I were wading the stream one day, and he did notice the cabin. I told him I'd ask Paul about it; he knew everything to be known about town affairs.

The storekeeper told me the unhappy story of the physician and his wife. "Doc would likely sell it," he mused. "I'll get you his address. You'd ought to write him and offer him . . . oh, five hundred dollars." I suspect now that Paul had a stake in the sale. He always seemed clever enough to see the main chance, and I've never thought to fault him simply for being so bright.

I did write the doctor, he asked a thousand, and we settled at $750. My brother-in-law and I both went in on the deal, and we have co-owned the place ever since, despite the fact that his sister and I divorced some thirteen years later along.

The cabin needed a great lot of work, but I took a novice's pleasure in seeing to much of that. I was a teacher, one of whose principal privileges has always been a long summer recess. My wife and I had no children in the early years, so, unlike my co-proprietor, I could spend a full three months by the river if I chose. And I did choose.

The table and the cabinetry in the camp are not of a sort to be found in a high-end catalog, but they remain serviceable. We bought an old woodstove from someone at the Passamaquoddy reservation, and got a pitcher pump from someone else to draw water out of the river. Creston installed a sink he'd found, God knows where, and built the counter to house it, a task beyond my meager capabilities; the counter was made moisture-resistant by means of yellow vinyl from the top of a junked Pontiac convertible. The fabric has lasted a lot longer than the car ever did. The first big upriver window we put in came from a hen coop.

So there were means of drinking, basic cooking, washing, and brushing our teeth; we had wood heat for chilly nights; we had crude beds and furniture; and we had an outhouse, which my former brother-in-law and I have always joked was the other one's share of our common ownership. The privy was *Peter's camp* or *Syd's camp,* depending on whether Syd or Peter spoke of it.

Things changed, of course, as things do with time's passage. Two children arrived, and the quick river and falls were persistent hazards for them. To worry about life-threatening accidents was to forfeit the very relaxation that those long academic vacations could otherwise foster.

If I feel a bit of the blues creeping in on me just now, I suppose that must have at least partly to do with the wreckage of that first marriage and the toll it was bound to have taken on those children, who were nine and four at the time of their parents' divorce. I'd showed myself far from a model father or husband, and I know it. My ex-wife was and remains a fine, courageous, and caring woman, and has been an extraordinary mother to the children she bore.

There's no wriggling out of accountability, but sometimes it seems to me that some law should have stopped me from making any marital commitment at twenty-three. I was a restless, hunting-and-fishing fool, not a grownup by anyone's standards.

I can't, however, make myself unwish that commitment, flimsy as it turned out to be, because that would be to unwish my wondrous oldest son and oldest daughter, who were already more adult in their teens than I in my late twenties; and it would also be to unwish the two children apiece they themselves now have, all of which is impossible to contemplate.

And I can't dismiss the fact, either, that—despite my post-adolescent turmoil of mind and heart—we experienced a fair share of joy in those early years, much of it having to do, precisely, with the ground on which I stand this morning. The children still have a relation to that ground, though my ex-wife's to a place she also deeply loved got sundered by our own sundering.

As I say, my parents already had a camp out in the lake that feeds this river, one far more commodious, far less perilous, especially as the kids grew ambulatory and then of course wildly active. The island increasingly became our own little family's refuge come summer. I used the river camp for the most part now as a studio. I'd go down early in the morning, write until noon, and return uplake at lunchtime, then down again after supper to fish whatever hatch might occur. In those days, you could skid on the bridge for the mayflies resting on the warm tar.

By the middle '70s—too soon, too soon—the river that for so long I'd shared with few others had become a destination for hordes of anglers. The extension of Interstate 95 all the way to Houlton had much to do with this. The river runs for a mere three and a half miles, and only about half of that, given the steep drop in its middle section, is really fishable. Idiot regulations (for decades you could kill an aggregate seven and a half pounds of landlocked salmon per day!), combined with growing pressure, conspired to decimate the electrifying wild fish. The prey would now be all but exclusively stocked.

Not that those stocked salmon couldn't grow big and feisty after a season or two, leaving the river for one of the lakes at either end in the hot months, fattening on smelt, returning the next spring. It was only that for me something had been taken out of the river forever. Of course there had always been stocked fish in that watershed, but now they almost completely crowded out the other kind.

Mainly, though, I just didn't like the idea of jostling for position amid a throng of people. I could get that sort of snarl, as if I'd ever want to, in some other place; I wouldn't look for it in remote Maine.

Needless to say, I'd been supremely spoiled. There were a lot of evenings when I sat in one of our Adirondack chairs beside the camp-yard fireplace, at which I'd just broiled a supper, and watched for rises.

"That looks like a good one," I'd mumble, and, setting my beer on a wooden arm, down I'd amble to flick a dry.

Those days were irretrievably gone, like so much else, and although there was no profit in lamenting them, I naturally did. I still do. At all events, apart from my writing hours, I now spent a week or so each year in the cabin, when I came north to pursue grouse and woodcock. Even in these later Junes, on fishing trips to the back lakes for smallmouth, to which I turned by default, I've stayed on the island, away from the mainland's vicious spring black flies.

And suddenly I'm here, ready to quit my teaching career, the last of five children—to my nagging pain, like a toothache's—having left our house. The four grandchildren have arrived, a great consolation, to be sure, but because we can't be with one or another son or daughter or grandson or granddaughter every day of the year, however we might want to be, it lately occurred to my wife and me that we might now visit the camp in off seasons, including the winter months. I hadn't done that in countless years. We'd explore on snowshoes or ski the lakes or just have time to ourselves in a hidden place.

I am, however, less and less enthusiastic as I age about staggering to an outdoor toilet in the middle of a sub-freezing night, even in October. January would, I knew, be out of the question for both of us. So, with permission from my co-owner, who, other commitments and allegiances interfering, hadn't set foot on the property for years anyhow, I decided to spruce things up.

There's a well now, and indoor plumbing, along with a bigger wood-stove and even a propane space heater, God save me, to keep the bathroom toasty if the fire should die. I hired a local builder for the whole job.

I stare upriver. Robin has been with me for a few days, but at noontime yesterday she headed back to work in Vermont. I already miss her, but I don't think her absence alone accounts for the wave of melancholy that has flooded my soul.

Aging beats the alternative. My poor father, who adored this territory about as much as I do, died of a massive coronary at fifty-six, Creston at the same age, and my immediately younger brother was felled by a brain aneurysm in his thirties. I have been more than comparatively lucky, no doubt about it—and yes, as I have often admitted and will again, even a spoiled one.

It's not the conceivable imminence of my own death or debilitation, however, that occasions this wistfulness. Or not exactly. Rather it's that, at sixty-eight, I believe at long last I know how to be a decent father, husband, friend, and now grandparent, at least most of the time. My chief regret is that, even if I live to a ripe age, I'll have had so little time to exercise what in my case must pass for wisdom.

It's obvious too how often I worry over never having adequately expressed my love for people now dead, the ones who occupy much of my attention in all these meditations. I even wonder if, filled with a young person's faith in worldly permanence, I properly loved this physical cabin, in all its crudeness, as I know how to do today—now that the crudeness has essentially vanished. Part of the definition of a camp, after all, is that it have no running water; so the place is not properly even a camp anymore, though I'm sure I'll persist in calling it so.

Too soon old, too late smart. That was a favorite saying of my grandmother, who lived well into her nineties. I paid no more attention to it back then than would any other red-blooded, self-serving punk of a kid. Today I understand, all too stingingly, what she meant.

By dint of will, I make myself think of the pleasures that await me and my wife in this tiny building and in the countryside around it. I see us paddling up Musquash Stream in late September, skiing out to Oxbrook Lake on one of those February days when the sky's blue is so deep it's almost navy, trekking up Wabassus Mountain and looking down on Third Lake in brilliant October.

No, I haven't yet adjusted to our empty nest, but I force thoughts of how downright cozy it will be, one of us sitting in that rocker, which I remember buying at a yard sale in Topsfield, the other in the armchair—all rodent-ravaged then—that I found and clumsily re-upholstered. The woodstove will be radiant, the night wind scattering snowflakes or stars, and that dear familiar, the river, humming under the ice in the flat, then vaulting out when it reaches Big Falls.

And yet.

And yet, perverse as it sounds, the carpenters and tradesmen having done their work so thoroughly and well, I do miss the scent of mouse urine and camphor balls; I miss the little gales whistling through gaps in the siding and window casings; I even miss going a full week without bathing as I chase the wildfowl, so that at trip's end I smell of sweat, of wood smoke and—the pointers having always shared my bed when I'm here alone in autumn—of gun dog.

I miss Creston and his uncle George MacArthur, to whom my family grew so close that we called him uncle too; I miss the wonderful raconteur Earl Bonness; I miss shrewd Paul Hoar, the storekeeper-guide who tipped us off to the place to begin with; I miss the days when Bea Bagley tended the post office, Bill White sold live bait and trained bird dogs, Glennister Brown ran the grader that swamped the rough road to this doorstep, Ada Chambers baked and sold her breads and pies out on Tough End, Hazel Rich tied exquisite streamer flies for the store, Eddie Brown—disabled by a logging accident—became a self-taught expert on the Passamaquoddy relics he constantly dug up. I could go on for ages and pages.

I miss these characters who in some cases lived in town well before electricity ever reached it, who worked in the woods prior to power saws, who cooked in log-fired ovens. The great drug television hadn't impoverished their narrative skills or their imaginations. They never sat in front of a screen and laughed out loud at comedians who, on their best days, were less funny than they on their worst. The elders once made their own, superior entertainment, mostly by way of telling stories.

I suddenly remember Uncle George on a thunder-stormy day. He sits at my table, tunelessly whistling and drumming his fingers, as he is given to do when he can't be out on the water, even though he is in his eighties on the morning I call up, even though he can't swim a stroke. The rain is like gunfire on the metal roof.

And what do I ask for?

"Tell me a story, George," I plead, as if I were an even younger kid.

George doesn't miss a beat. "We cut cedar one winter right across there." He gestures to the tossing woods behind Mink Rock, as if actual landmarks could start a yarn, as in fact they usually could.

"There was a fella worked with us. He was called Stubby, on account of being so short, and he had a hunched back. Worked like the rest of us, and done as well as a sound man. The Devil was, he couldn't tell time."

George looks at his own wristwatch, affecting a puzzled expression.

"The boss bought him an alarm clock, so he could quit for dinner and that, but of course us boys would get ahold of the thing after the boss set it, and we'd twist it just anyhow. Poor Stub wouldn't know was it ten in the morning or four in the afternoon if the sun wasn't shining."

I see Uncle George shake his head in some odd mix of self-reproach, nostalgia, and amusement.

"In them days Robbie Sutherland run the store. He and a woman named Mrs. Hawkins lived down handy the falls here. They was both fond of a drink, and when they got feeling too good, the fur would certainly fly.

"One night, they started in to feud, and this Mrs. Hawkins, she grabs a clock off the table and takes Robbie right over the ear with it."

George pantomimes Robbie's shocked reaction to the blow, standing up to weave and stagger, to do it right.

"Next day, Robbie's in his store with a big bandage around his head, which probably wouldn't feel all that good even *without* this fracas with the clock. Stub comes to the door with that alarm clock in his hand, and he calls in, 'Hey, storekeeper, what time you got?'

"Robbie don't even look over at Stubby but only says, 'You go to hell, you humpback son of a bitch!'"

It's still a good story. I love to repeat it, as I suspect I repeat a lot of stories nowadays. In fact, I know I do. Sometimes when she hears me say, "I can't remember if I've told you this," our youngest child will answer before I've uttered a word, "Yes, Dad, you have."

But for me certain stories will always bear retelling; I recite them to myself almost daily, as if I were the last on earth who could understand them, as it can sometimes feel I am.

I go on to remember Earl Bonness sitting at the same table, in a longer siege of poor weather. It has rained for two weeks straight. The cabin perches on ledge, and I have to wade to my truck as surely as I'd be wading the river if the downpour would just let up. I've invited Earl over for what we call "a tap."

I'm only in my twenties, and have all the pretension of an aspirant adult. I've brought along a bottle of finest single malt Scotch whiskey. I pour my friend a drink. This is expensive stuff, so it is not as big a serving as he's used to, or wants.

Earl turns the jug's label toward him, reads it out loud, "Fifteen years old . . . "

"Fifteen years," I proudly echo.

"Small for his age," Earl muses.

A high-handed wind has come on, turning the flat of Big Falls Pool to whitecaps, which resemble a flock of scattering, terrified lambs. That blow won't do the grouse hunting much good, especially for a man like me, whose hearing has worsened with time and gunfire. But I've always loved a bracing day like this on the stream. As I step outside, I feel one of those nameless, nagging aches—in my hip this time—that come every so often now, and so far always go away. I also inhale the wind-borne odors, each a tonic again: evergreen perfume, smoke, musty duff of the forest floor, clean savory spray. My knees buckle, but not with physical pain.

Bird dog Pete yawns and whines at once, his body a shiver head to tail. Like all his predecessors, he's impatient with my human slowness, more pronounced in these later years. He suddenly looks the spitting image of Hector, my very first grouse dog, sun rebounding off his flanks. I shake my head to clear it. Where am I?

A flight of Goldeneye arrives in a sudden hurtle and plows into the pool above the falls, almost without setting wings. The birds scurry under the cutbanks on either side, leaving lathers of wake that will be hauled downstream to break up among the rapids. It's as if the ducks were fleeing from something.

As they may be. An eagle, its white parts fore and aft blazing under the early light, rips toward me and my dog, very low. Noticing us in the camp yard, at the last minute the raptor banks and soars up over the gold-leafed popples on the west shore.

I decide to take this frantic ballet of ducks and this glissade of eagle as auguries, and promising ones. The river is still emphatically there. My cabin, in whatever shape, abides at its edge. My dog, like all before, looks yearningly at the crate in the bed of my pickup, squealing his avidity. I still seem to feel it too.

Daybook, October

The heavens have teemed all day today. I've sat here by the woodstove, alternately dozing and reading Edward Arlington Robinson, the darkness of the poetry and the darkness of the day complementing each other so perfectly as to make an aesthetic experience—which lightens the darkness. And how snug it's been in this little Maine cabin anyhow, with the autumn-low river's purr outside the window, the rainfall's tattoo on the standing seam roof.

No matter the self-contempt I'd once have felt on admitting as much, it's a pleasure not to be out there hiking and hunting. I've been at that all day for almost a week, and I'm not shy anymore to confess that the old bones and muscles savor the respite.

I keep falling in and out of sleep in my chair. During one of the wakeful spells, I had a look at the bird-hunting log I started in the early '70s. I used to come here with my friends Terry and Joe, the former of whom got hooked on archery for deer and permanently abandoned our grouse outings, while the latter moved to Colorado.

The book tells me that for almost two decades, it was routine for us to bag forty grouse in five or six days. Twenty-five was a number we logged with disappointment, likewise any trip in which all three of us had not limited—twelve birds—on at least one of those days.

Our team shot a lot of woodcock in those earlier times too, but the little birds drop out of the log around 1984. Having seen their numbers dwindle, we'd all decided to let them fly by then, unless we were working a green dog, in which case we would shoot one or two, provided the points had been steady.

I have not shot a single ruffed grouse here this year.

Sad truth is, I've had next to no opportunity to do so, their numbers so wretchedly scanty and what few I've found so restive they won't hold for the point at all. Wild flushes. Tree birds.

What happened? This countryside is not like so many of my old Vermont and New Hampshire haunts, which have either grown up into big woods or been finished off by so-called development, the newcomer owners completely obliterating the game's habitat for lawns and meadows, and then—believing they help that game—posting their land, on which no true wildlife now exists or can. No, great oceans of unspoiled cover remain up here, so it's not a matter of habitat. What happened?

Something ominous.

There are those who believe that massive spraying for spruce budworm eliminated not only those larvae but also a lot of the other grubs that grouse chicks so desperately need for protein. But the spraying program ceased almost twenty years ago, and it wouldn't account anyhow for the skinny numbers in such Vermont covers as still have all the makings, because Vermont didn't get that spraying.

Something ominous.

I'm not dismayed by my personal lack of luck, as I would have been back when those old entries were made; I don't need to fill up my game pocket anymore to enjoy a hunt. It's all about the dog work and the hard walking. No, I'm disturbed, precisely, for the dog, and more so for the birds, whose absence implies something dire. What have we done to our planet? And I do mean *we:* I came here by car, not horseback, after all.

There are days when I thank God that I'm no longer so young as the man who wrote in that bird log, the world become a place where iconic creatures like the grouse must struggle so grimly to endure.

On the other hand, I have five children. And on the other hand, I have four grandchildren.

Eighty Percenters:
Reflections on Grouse
and Grouse Dogs*

It's late into the north country's grouse season. The covers have gone spare; the peak foliage has long since tumbled. I like it this way, the leaves' early splendor given over, the far ridges abstract, hard-edged. You may, like me, have the illusion that your mind has cleaned up a little too, the summer clutter blown out. Impossible, of course, not to mourn a bit. This clarity, this grandest part of the shotgun season, is so temporary.

Gus is among the finest grouse dogs I've handled. I got him at nine months from a professional breeder-trainer in northern Maine, who predicted he'd be a "wild Indian." That sounded good to me for a lot of reasons. Mostly, it sounded as if, like a lot of grouse gunners, no doubt the majority in fact, the handler had the usual sense of what made a good pointing dog in our region. My subject here, really, is how misguided I believe that sense can be, as the following anecdote—on my word of honor, a true one—indicates. But in all candor, I may not even be talking of dog handling at all in this account. We'll see about that.

It's been a relatively poor year for birds. By my records, they peaked in 1976, when, under licenses from three states, we shot a bird for each

---

This, in minimally revised form, is the oldest essay in the present collection; I include it in part to remember the sort of hunter I was, which is both continuous with and different from the one I am today. I hope at least that some of the young one's immodesty has abated, as I know his youthful physical energies have.

year of the century. I don't know how that stacks up against tallies in the Midwest or in West Virginia, say, but around here, where the season is scarcely over a month long, seventy-six grouse among three hunters is a hell of a year.

On this late afternoon, we are about halfway through the decline from that summit to the bottoming out that will come in '84, when we'll still manage thirty partridge, but oh, how we'll work for them!

We've worked hard enough even today. Gus is tall and lean and very active, four years old now, getting better every season; but in all his hearty ranging since this morning, he's locked up just twice, and we're fifty percent. I can replay that miss, or misses, on the first flush: right out straightaway, along a brook bed, no obstructions, *bang* and *bang*. Gone! I can't believe it!

Well, yes I can. So can you if you're a grouse hunter.

The two points came early, my miss and Joe's kill, a sweet over-the-shoulder shot on a cinnamon hen. Since then, it's been a lot of tramping in steep country, and if we three were not such friends it's almost sad, or if we were other than young, Joe and Terry and I might have called it quits by now.

In fact we are more or less headed home when we pass a corner where we know of one apparently lead-proof grouse. Just one. The cover is tiny, and we like to bust brush for at least an hour at a time when we get out of the truck, so we haven't run through this patch for quite a spell. But the last day of the season looms, and we don't like one-grouse hunts at any point in the fall. We'll try for a second bird here.

There's a hedge of skinny pines just as you step in. Then it's a meadow with popple whips all through it, and a few twisty apples at the uphill end before it breaks into open hardwoods by an old beagle club's abandoned shack. There's a headstone a few hundred yards into those hardwoods. One John Goodridge lies under it. I wrote a lousy poem about that grave once. I couldn't help it.

I pull the crate's door at the back of the pickup, and Gus leaps onto the dirt. He takes four strides and huddles up in his customary crapping posture, quivering all the while, high-headed, nostrils working. We call it The Kennel Point. It doesn't matter how many times in the day he's done this, how many covers we've hit; he's got to have that kennel point before we go in.

I don't like him spraddled in the road that way; I keep an ear out for cars coming. Even he is impatient with his rite. In fact, just now he's whining, staggering toward the pine-strip in the act, leaving a trail of dung balls like Hansel's crumbs. He looks like a man hobbling back to camp from the privy, having forgotten the toilet paper, except that his nose is low as he waddles along.

We joke about Gus's behavior, pay it no real attention, wander ahead of him into the woods to wait for him. Joe almost steps on the grouse, which whirrs out through the softwood and heads somewhere up toward that dilapidated shack. We exchange the standard head-shaking curses, and Terry as usual says, "We should have minded the dog for once." We'll try to chase the bird up; it shouldn't have gone too far. There's not much place to go, and no one fired his gun.

Now here's the point at which many a hunter who ought to know better will check his dog, even have him, poor animal, trot along at heel or sit in the car, so as not to bump the grouse he knows is in there somewhere.

I have not checked Gus. He hasn't heard me say, "Whoa!" all day. I haven't said a thing to him now but "All Right!" meaning Go Ahead.

So it hasn't been two minutes, but my dog has been through the whole cover, ranging anywhere from underfoot to maybe 120 yards out. And now he's locked on. No bell. That's our bird, I'm sure, and I'm sure there aren't any others in this patch.

But where in hell *is* the bird? Where in hell is Gus? "Oh, there!" Joe calls, after we've searched for more than just a few minutes; he waves a hand toward the edge of the big woods. Gus's point is solid, picture-perfect, I wish I had a camera. Or maybe I'm glad I don't. I have that embarrassing miss to atone for, the birds are pretty rare this year, I want to shoot something beside a photograph. It's getting on dusk.

We approach as we always do. I'm in the middle. Terry's on my left, Joe on the right, each of them slightly ahead of me to guard the corners, keep the grouse inside. We've done this over so many points that we don't have to talk anymore.

Soon, though, we begin to talk a lot, our squadron collapsing into itself around the dog, who hasn't moved an inch, still stands there stiff as a spike and trembling.

"False point," I mutter, irked. I could have the best dog in the state, but he'd never be quite good enough. That's what Terry tells me. He's the one mellowing influence on our outings, a ballast to the huff that we others sometimes bring along.

"Talk about a hunt!" Joe growls, grouchy as I am.

I'm ready to give Gus a little nudge with my boot, because he won't leave it alone, this patch of perfectly open ground, all pallid beech leaves and umber oak.

"Now just a minute," says Terry. He always does. I love him like a brother, but his laconic demeanor in moments like this sometimes makes me half want to cuff him. "Be ready," he warns.

Joe and I look at each other, sneering, rolling our eyes, as Terry walks a couple of concentric loops around the point. We've already done that! Nothing, again. Maybe a woodcock, Terry may be thinking. He kicks the hardhack ten yards ahead. Nothing. He grins; he knows what Joe and I are thinking about him, and he's good for it.

Then we all watch Gus's head droop earthward, slow as a second hand. At the very last instant, we also see the bird, another brown phase grouse, wings spread, flattened to the woods floor, which almost precisely matches its coloration. Panic, of course. I tense, stammer something inscrutable to my partners, lay my finger along the trigger guard. But by now Gus has simply picked up the shocked bird and, with two strides, he's holding it out for me. I tonk its head against a small tree.

Not a shot, mind you, has been fired.

You may say that this partridge was pricked up by some hunter in here before us, but I think you'll be wrong, not only because we've never seen signs of another person here but also because I take a full twenty minutes dressing that grouse, picking its feathers right up over the head, holding the body at all angles in the truck's high beam. Not a dent, not a scratch.

Did it stun itself on a branch or whatever? Maybe. But I'm all but certain that the bird was sound as a dollar, and that Gus, bold, fast and high-headed, simply froze it on that open ground. The critter had nowhere to hide, was perhaps caught in its dash between tangles, and the dog simply pinned it.

I believe as much not because Gus has ever before pulled this stunt, but because any number of times he has come so close. We've all found him, two to five feet from a grouse, looking it right in the eye, such that at length we too can see the bird as plain as day, motionless. He is famous for these tight points, though I take no particular credit. I didn't "do" anything. If there's credit coming to me, in fact, it's for *not* doing a lot. I let him go. I always let them go.

I don't take much credit for that either, since I learned such permissiveness when I was a kid from an older man, one of the best upland hunters you could want to meet. I'll call him Jack; he never wanted his name, let alone his hunting grounds, identified in print, and I honor that insistence even after his death.

Jack was dour, even rude. He made those Yankee-quick judgments on anyone he bumped into. The one he made on me, within the first five minutes of our acquaintance, turned out positive. Don't ask me why.

I was running my first very own bird dog then. Hector was in his third season, and I had pretty well settled him down, as the jargon has it. He worked good and close, to keep borrowing the conventional terms. He whoa'd at a whisper. I liked that, was proud of it, and I was irritated on my first hunt with my new friend that whenever my dog got out more than forty yards from me, I'd whistle him around, and Jack would shout, in a high-pitched voice, as if he were talking to a baby, "*He's* all right!" Sure he was all right; he bumped two birds, and the three that went down were birds that Jack flushed as he raced up on points way over in his direction. Meanwhile, I got skunked.

Jack's own dog, a stylish little setter bitch named Millie (I use a pseudonym even for her), had cut herself badly early in the season, so we had to wait for a late October day before we left Hector at home to see what she could do. Which was plenty. I'd never known a dog of any breed that located so many grouse as this one, but she made you labor for them. Or she and Jack together did.

I was in college then, hunting weekends only, drinking my share of beer, chubby and out of shape. Millie operated like no one's idea of a grouse dog that I'd heard about, and Jack urged her to it. We might have been on horseback at some quail plantation. I wished we were, because in that hilly country it was about all I was worth to keep up with the older man as he kept up with his dog. I'd never witnessed anything like it. Often as not, we'd spend more time hunting far off somewhere for her point than Millie herself had spent coming to it. But she held her birds. Jack killed a limit, and I shot three.

Sure, she and I and Jack among us probably bumped that many, or they bumped themselves. But we chased up three of those. They were among the ones we shot over steady points. I couldn't at first understand why her owner would just let Millie rush over to the mark at her own galloping free will, but that's what he did, and by God it worked!

And that's what I have done with my own dogs ever since. Hector never really got the habit. Too late. He remained slow by my revised standards, and by Jack's he was "a vacuum cleaner," one of the snide terms he reserved for such deliberate workers. Another was "sniffer."

My next, Sam, was faster. The first Wes faster still. Gus the fastest, but my later bitch, Annie, was a close second, and I wish I could have bred her to Gus.

Give me a quick, high-headed dog.

Jack's setter was calm enough on the ride home, so long as we stayed on pavement. On the dirt stretches in between, she'd yelp and whine until she drove me almost nuts. She wanted to go hunting, and the rougher roads made her think we were about to, though dark had fallen.

"Pretty eager," I said.

"Better be," said Jack.

Millie came from one of the fanciest bloodlines in the South. A local retiree of means had paid almost a thousand bucks for her in the late '50s—a real price for a gun dog in those days—but the old fellow just couldn't handle her. She was too high-energy; she wouldn't whoa; he couldn't stay with her. He had come to Jack for advice. Most people did. Jack had been dogless himself for a brief while, so he offered an opinion, provided he could take the prospect out alone and look her over. The owner hemmed and hawed—this was expensive flesh—but finally consented. Jack returned in an hour or so with Millie, two woodcock and two grouse. The old man blinked.

"What did you do?"

"Didn't do nothin'. You got the best dog in the neighborhood, I'd judge." The old man blinked again. "Trouble is, you're just too used up to suit her. That's all."

I told you he was rude.

The long and short of it is that Jack got Millie for free, and the grouse paid dearly until, at no less than fourteen, she finished her last season and died soon after. Maybe we all ought to give our bird dogs snowshoe hares for feed, the way he did.

"A dog has a pace," Jack told me on the way home from that shoot nearly fifty years back. "Up to you to stay with it, not the other way round." He was hunting the roadside with his eyes from the car, even as the night grew deep.

"Fast is the way, I say," he muttered, and I felt a touch of his contempt for my own obvious exhaustion and unfitness.

Of course Jack's words, spare as they were, fly directly into the face of the usual wisdom: that a dog must adapt to the *hunter's* pace, which means, in four-legged terms, he must slow down and he'd better stay close. It also means that if he gets scent he'd better start thinking *Whoa!* He'd better start to sneak. You don't want him to bump that bird!

This leads to the first among several difficulties resulting from that alleged wisdom. I mean false pointing, a habit I detest, but not one I've been much plagued by since the days with Hector, who occasionally practiced it. I let my dogs know it's okay to make a mistake, just as long as they're hunting, really hunting. Lord knows I make mistakes myself. Don't remind me of that straightaway up the brook, of the scores of others like it, when the dogs were solid, fine, nothing to blame *them* for.

Once you get a dog truly worried about running over a bird, he's going to lock up on the first thing that stinks: an old grouse wallow, a pecked apple gone brown at the edges, not to mention, as I've seen, early season turtles, chipmunks, hares, and even, once, a dead pig in an abandoned well. And when your dog does have it right, when there *is* a grouse in the cover, he's going to freeze at the first whiff. Then you and your buddies are going to try to sneak up, and the grouse is going to thunder away far in front of you, out of range, and you're going to believe you're better off hunting this particular game with no dog at all.

Joe and Terry are known for truthful men. Ask them if you don't believe me. *About eighty percent of the grouse we flush are ones that the dog has located.* By this I mean that of course there are some which she or he has begun to work but hasn't locked up on. Maybe the wind has made the game hawky, or, as I swear is the case, a low population has made them so. But these trailing points or soft points are the exceptions. In the first season for one of my dogs, we don't shoot over these "locations" at all, much less shooting at birds that one of us bumps himself.

I'm a selfish hunter, and—however badly it reflects on my character—never a casual one. I'm in it for something other than what's called recreation, something a little like religion, I think, a rather stern, radical-Protestant variety, because hunting for me has something, God knows why, to do with a dim notion of saving my soul.

My circle of regular hunting companions, therefore, have been the precious few, and I do mean precious, who feel the same way, including Terry, for all his easy-going manner. I mention this because I've been acquainted with a much wider circle of "hunters" who've dismissed my claims about proportion of kills to points as simple bragging. But I know from the way they talk how they hunt and handle their dogs, and I've never meant to invite them along to see the truth of my claims. We come from antithetical camps, nice as many of these folks indisputably are.

Furthermore, I've never been in competition when I hunt, except with the game, and with some fabricated ideal of myself. As Jack used to say, "Let 'those people' do as they please. They won't cause the birds any harm anyhow." Why should I care how they find their fun?

Good thing we get those eighty percent points. Some of my small company are consistently expert shots, but none on the regular team—Terry, Joe, and I—shoot like Landy Bartlett over in Sunderland, none like Jack before macular degeneration got him and he had to give up wing shooting, none like my pal Peter Woerner. No, we've been among the truly successful grouse hunters in the region less for spectacular gunning than for our shared convictions about a dog's moves, and about each other's. If we didn't mean to let our dogs go, to honor their paces, we'd use flushers, which of course *must* work close.

A certain number of grouse, again, are going to flush wild, dog or no dog. Everyone who hunts them knows what it is to hear the faint explosion of wings a hundred yards away, before you've said a word, before you've taken a step into cover. We know how common is the opposite. It's late, you're tired, the sidehill is steep; you stand around the truck, joking with one another, razzing, whooping, putting off that damned slope with its razor hawthorns and clotted hardhack for another few minutes. At last you plough in, up and back, never a bird—not until you've slipped your guns into their cases, whereupon the bird that had sat downwind, right next to the road, while you tramped away uphill and back, will scare you to death, clapping into the woods.

But the woods are dark now. Time to get home to food and family. And so you head back, that good tiredness in your bones, a mess of game, if you've had the luck, stiffening in the bed of the pickup, the barn lights in the fields off the highway blinking, exotic as stars. You are quiet. You've already gone through the banal repartee.

Terry: "Imagine that son of a bitch! He sat there the whole time!"

Joe: "Waited till we made all our noise and shot holes in the sky at that woodcock."

I: "Who'd believe it?"

We three would believe it. It's happened to us so often, and to you too, no? Or you've been slogging around through a prime part of the cover; the dog has some vague notion, but there isn't anything here. You've been back and forth through it three times. Man and dog alike stop and take a breather by that deadfall. That's precisely when the tree grouse thunders out.

What to make of all this?

I'm not doctrinaire about what to make of it, because I can be as wrong as the next person, but I'll tell you what Joe and Terry and I have concluded over the years. *Always be alert,* you think, but no. That'll never happen, and we might as well face it. What we've made of it is very simple, that if a number of grouse will flush wild, period, a certain number won't.

In any event, you are not going to creep up on a grouse, no matter how careful you are. You just can't do such a thing if you hunt the textbook cover of mixed hard- and softwood, feed, dense understory. Daniel Boone couldn't surprise an ox in there. Your dog's not going to surprise a grouse, either, not with that bell around his neck anyway. (I guess it's an implicit opinion here that if you have a dog that doesn't need some device to let you hear him, a bell in the days I recall, perhaps a beeper now, you have a dog *you* don't need.)

So let him go. Let yourself go. Move! Call back and forth to one another, because it's not just a matter of safety; you want to be in position when the grouse takes off. If there are three of you, and one of you on the flank has lagged behind, that's the corner the bird will spill out of, right?

A lot of grouse behavior is mysterious. Think of Crazy Flight in autumn. This is why this game bird is so much fun and such a challenge to hunt; it's why, as well, speculation on that bird is usually just speculation. Though here I'm talking chiefly about things I've inferred from observation, from trial and a whole lot of error, I like to speculate as much as you do.

For example, a grouse at feed in the daytime has to be on guard not only against bloodthirsty types like us and other earthbound predators but also against killers in the air. Three times in my life I've had raptors finish off grouse I'd winged, once in mid-flight.

That stooping hawk is deadly, not least because it *can* by God sneak up; so our grouse is a little reluctant to fly. He's heavy, his wings are short, and it's a lot easier on him to go on foot and stay undercover. He'd rather hide from a red tail or broad wing than try to outrace him above ground.

And again, he can *hear* whatever approaches on the ground. If it's the odd daytime bobcat or fox, he can wait until the last minute and hop up into a tree like Lafontaine's crow. If it's some clumsy hunter, he can size up the guy's movements and then as we all know fly off at just the right height and angle to leave the gunner with his teeth in his mouth or cursing over the spent shells at his feet.

The grouse isn't nervous, really. He's not afraid. Or if he is, it's not the fear that we would feel in his place. Like every creature low on the food chain, he's a professional. The thing that makes him jumpy is that damned quiet. That's a reason, it seems to me, for the flightiness of any game on a windy day—it's too hard to tell by sound where the danger lies.

Our hunter has just hissed *whoa,* if that's possible, his dog has come to a halt, everybody's trying to figure out how to tiptoe forward and surprise the partridge—which of course doesn't know any of this. All he knows is that it's gotten scary quiet. Where have those stalkers gone? Time to get the hell out of here, which he does. Now the sportsmen start trying to blame one another, or shaking their heads in resignation to the fact that there just isn't any good way to hunt ruffed grouse, except maybe to set snares on the drumming logs.

And so I repeat my heresy: Let the dog go. I go, he goes, she goes, we all go. If the bird is determined to scram without stopping to think the matter over, so be it. At least we'll know he was there. Maybe we can get a line on him for a second flush. Maybe, as so often, after a wild flight he'll be as tight now as he was spooky on the first flush. If the dog bumps him by mistake, or because of bad conditions, that's all right too. Again, we know he was there, as we mightn't have otherwise, and we'll try to follow him up yet a third time. And so on.

But we won't, on this flush or the next or next or next, jangle that bird's nerves by vainly attempting a silent approach. We aren't hawks. We and the dog will move at a fast pace, and—who knows?—one of these days our bird dog may pull Gus's old trick, and none of us will have to shoot and miss.

Eight locations to ten flushes. Not perfect. Here I'll join for a moment in the conventional wisdom's chorus and say that, no, there is no perfect grouse dog. A certain proportion of the birds are going to fool you and fool your dog, at which point Terry, or someone like him, if you're lucky enough to have one for a partner, will risk being pummeled by the Joes and Syds among you for speaking the truth: "Well, that's what makes it interesting." But if you thought you could have a dog who was that consistent on grouse, I bet you'd try to get that dog somehow.

A fair amount of what I say is really not completely a matter of dog work, after all. It's up to you. Are you a person who would turn down a free trip to the Bahamas in order to shoot a limit of partridge, or try? Then you have a good chance, following my permissive methods, of having such a pointing dog, because you'll kill some game. And that above all is the important thing for your companion.

You'll kill game because you and he will be in the cover at every possible opportunity, because you'll make time in order to do so, let other things slide. You can't shoot them from your office. I have always had it easy, I admit, as a college professor; as I rose through the ranks, I managed to get a lighter and lighter autumn teaching load. If I made up for that in the spring, that was okay; the trout fishing didn't really pick up until school was out anyhow.

Are you willing to get yourself into better shape than I was on that pivotal day with Jack? You should, because as he said, and as I affirm, it's a matter of determining and honoring the dog's pace, not the other way round. As the season goes on, this will come easier. You'll shed that summer roll and you'll get your eye in as well as it can be gotten in.

And the grouse will sit better—again despite the conventional wisdom—as the brush gets spare. As I say, given a choice, most ruffs want to stay out of the air. If there are plenty of early leaves and brush, however, they're apt to fly off through that good protection, more apt than when, as on that austere day when Gus picked up the live cinnamon, there's nothing between them and the dreadful gray sky but this tuft of browned weed, those clumps of steeple-bush, this camouflage barrier of gorgeous feathers, almost invisible, so closely has God matched them to the woodsy colors of my off-season dreams.

Blessed

A dog you love should live as long as you do.

How often now have I said this to myself since I began hunting over dogs? That was fifty-nine years ago, when I toted my single-shot .410 on some of my father's shorter forays into the field. At nine, I didn't shoot much game, but when at long last his gun dog died, I recall—more vividly than I do most things from that time—how I protested the plain injustice of it all. Like a father, a dog was surely meant to endure forever.

I have grieved for a lot of dogs since, in ways quintessentially similar to that first time. For Hector, who had that uncanny knack of pointing up at a limb-perched grouse, who still inhabits the brush of memory. For the first Wes, whose toothy smile and plain honesty so endeared him to me. For Gus, who shines with sleet in my mind's eye—a certain fabulous late October hunt, no matter the foul weather, near my Maine cabin.

Bessie. Sam. Annie. Belle. Wes II. And those are only the pointing dogs. There are the retrievers too, somewhat fewer but no less dear.

I recall reading an article in some dreary pop-psych mag, as a person may do in dentists' or optometrists' waiting rooms. Its thesis was that two weeks at most comprised a person's span of heartache after a dog dies, which was at least more than the single week the cat-lovers got. The author of that piece, I suspect, never owned a dog, or at least not a working one, just as so many child-rearing experts—Locke, stock, and Piaget—have never been parents. Maybe I'm the exception who proves the rule, though

I doubt it, but I for one think sorrowfully of all my gun dogs, and I've done so a lot over the decades.

And joyfully too. It's not only that I can summon grand old days with each, and some comical ones, and frustrating too, but I also recognize that if one of those adored dogs had in fact lived as long as I have, there'd be only the one to adore. *Death is the mother of beauty,* as poet Wallace Stevens famously put it, and true enough, the athleticism, the grace, the quirky personality of every one of my dogs burned themselves into my consciousness, and at length into my remembrance, not least because in my soul I understood how briefly I'd get to treasure them.

In my most heartbreaking dreams, however, I never imagined that Wes II's life would prove so fleeting. A foursquare muscle merchant with the heart of a bull, he seemed as solid as earth itself. When, having just turned seven years old, he came up lame one morning, I took him to our veterinarian, foreseeing perhaps a few doses of Metacam, and then we'd go back to business as usual.

We had just returned from eastern Montana, after all, where for six five-hour days we'd stalked the Huns and sharptails and ringnecks of the high prairie, and where Wes had seemed nothing but Wes until the last day. Uncharacteristically, he pottered a lot that morning, but I figured only that five rugged hunts in a row had worn him down, made him footsore.

"He's been hiding this from you for a long time," said our good vet Diane, "and I can't see how." The x-ray showed shadow in his left shoulder where bone should have been, the cancer that ravenous. It seemed nothing could be done.

A surgeon's second opinion more or less matched hers. He did propose that we might right then and there do a radical amputation, but he was honest enough to predict an extra six months at best as a result. I couldn't imagine this stout creature as a tripod. I drove home in tears.

As it turned out, Wes lived that six months, and several more, without any surgery. I got word of Nate Heinemann, a Cornell-trained veterinarian over in Burlington, who incorporated traditional Chinese medicine into his practice. The doctor's acupuncture, a dietary change and some herbs—together, to be sure, with Western narcotics—erased my dog's limp overnight, and gave him if anything a little too much energy; I feared that bum shoulder would snap at any moment. But like the other two consultants,

Nate knew the game would soon be up. He cautioned that his own treatment would work no miracles, would be palliative, not curative.

Virtually all the pointers I've trained and hunted have had one thing in common: they've been almost as unenthusiastic about swimming as your average pussycat. But Wes plain craved the water. Every July, when my family arrived at our island camp, which sits on a nine-mile lake, he'd rush out to the end of the dock and—like a champion Lab, all four feet high in the air—make his entry. He would then paddle around for actual hours. No need of September roadwork to harden him up for bird season; by the time we got back to Vermont, Wes was nothing but gristle.

Not so long ago, that good dog's ashes floated away from the dock.

I am barely a twentieth-century man, let alone a twenty-first. So my eventual recourse was entirely unlike me: I searched the Internet for a pup whose genetic makeup was as close to Wes's as I could find. I didn't necessarily desire another Aquadog, but at my advancing age I did want one equally biddable if possible, an ace in the field and also a good guy to hang out with in New England's much too long off-season.

I was looking above all for a scion of Snakefoot, one of the many champions in the Elhew line developed by the late Bob Wehle. I have heard some call Elhews the most over-rated dogs in America and others call them the contrary. One thing they are is famously tractable, not a thing always said about pointers. Indeed there are wags who claim that the breed got its name because, asked a question like "Where's your dog?" an English owner's frequent response would be to point into the distance, toward, say, the coast of France.

I have had four Elhew pointers, two brilliant and, to jump ahead, a third prospectively so. Each of these was a Snakefoot descendant.

The odd one out in this list was lovable, eccentric—and not a good gun dog. Nor was he a Snakefooter. Yet I hold myself rather than genes chiefly responsible for Max's hopelessness; I failed to recognize him early enough for the soft dog he turned out to be. I therefore very probably and stupidly raised my voice one too many times, not so much at him as at his hardheaded and fearless kennel-mate bitch (non-Elhew), the result being that he'd start off like a champion, and then, fearful of chastisement, he'd more or less quit hunting. That example should be a warning, which I've tried ever since to heed myself, to anyone who thinks of pointers as somehow bomb-proof. Most of mine have been, but by ill temper I may well have squandered the considerable talent of the one who wasn't.

I suspect my inclination to the genetic strain that resulted in Wes (and his predecessor Belle)—like many if not most dog-related inclinations—involves its share of superstition. Be that as it may, my search took me to a kennel in Arizona, of all places, and I picked my pup on the basis of a photograph alone.

That was in December, but by airline restrictions the new dog couldn't be shipped until weather warmed up, which in our north country meant May. This gave me some interlude, likewise, to brace my wife—as in my cravenness I hadn't yet done, Wes still deceptively hale—for the addition of a fourth dog to our pack. In short, I never met Pete, as my youngest daughter, who names all our dogs, dubbed him, until he'd already reached nine months of age. Not ideal, but it would have to do.

I liked what I saw the minute I uncrated him at Bradley Airport down in Connecticut. He was not so blocky as his predecessor, but he had an even deeper chest, so deep that to someone unfamiliar with the breed it might even look freakish. Oh, but he was a handsome specimen—except that he had pretty bad dentition, an under-bite so pronounced that at times his whole lower arch would jut out and cover his top lip. With a fairly short muzzle, Pete's countenance looked in such moments as much like a boxer's as a pointer's.

Perhaps the breeder should have warned me of this defect, even discounted his asking price, and yet, like the rest of my family, I have come to delight in Pete's sudden changes of aspect. Just now he looks as though he belongs on the cover of *Pointing Dog Journal,* and now he looks like a cartoon goofball. His ill-placed teeth, I thought, might have an unanticipated advantage: he'd not be able to chew up any birds in his maiden hunts, even should he want to, as it turned out he did not; but I get ahead of myself.

There have been times in late years when I almost believed the disease that brought the second Wes low to be somehow contagious. I had too many friends, hunters and non-hunters alike, who were losing their own dogs to cancer. But more importantly, there were humans in my life who confronted its horrors. My noble and generous pal of forty-plus years, Strachan Donnelley, would die of a stomach tumor around the time of Pete's first birthday; the hilarious and moving poet Jack Myers had survived other cancers but was now waiting for a liver transplant down in Texas, his last chance; a lovely local woman, Ellen Ryan, had passed on the winter before from cancer; and my cherished brother-in-law, a Massachusetts police officer, was recuperating from yet another brutal round of chemotherapy while I trained my pup.

What brother-in-law Chip has taught me—and what, at the risk of sounding preachy, I think all of us should bear in mind, as we rarely do— is that, in his own words, every day alive is a good one. After his first bout with cancer and its hideous treatment six years before, he described raking his front lawn and musing on how lousy a chore it once seemed. Now he asked himself, "How could I ever have thought that?"

I mention all this because last summer, as I worked young Pete on quail from a bird launcher and on a few released pheasant, and as I deeply felt the loss of Wes, frequently even calling the new dog by the old one's name, the illness and suffering of my wife's brother were much on my mind. His case reminded me, and scarcely for the first time in my lucky life, that I was and am a blessed soul, and that I therefore must cling to what and more importantly whom I love. All that seems so durable can vanish in a heartbeat.

Even with so cooperative a pointer as Pete, I had my exasperations, as anyone who has started a dog from scratch knows there must be. A young dog breaking a point on a bird, however, and cutting rope-burns into the palm that held the check cord—well, it wasn't drinking a liquid that proved either hotter or colder than a certain prescribed temperature and thus feeling as though your mouth were full of razor blades. It wasn't watching the skin of your arms and legs flake up and peel from the flesh, your veins turning to grim black tattoos. It wasn't going cold turkey from the Oxy-Contin without which you couldn't have borne your pain.

Once, when my wife praised Chip for battling cancer with chemo-therapy, he wrote that there was no fight involved; you just took the mauling. "It's like having two thugs show up at your house, tie you to a chair, then beat the shit out of you all afternoon. A week later, when you're starting to feel okay, they show up and do it again."

I've always been intrigued and gratified by training dogs, but now to steady Pete to flush and shot seemed an utter luxury, a sort of grace that I didn't merit or have to, any more than good Chip deserved his illness and the wretched treatment it invited.

My wife reminds me that every new dog I start is my favorite ever. She's likely right. There may well be some sort of psyche-preserving mechanism at work in me to make that so. I must therefore be skeptical of myself, must stop short of saying, after this rather brief time with the new man, that Pete's my best of all time. He may go south in his sophomore season. I've seen it happen. All I can say for now is that he's at least the quickest study I have ever handled.

I try to keep my commands to any working dog as few and simple as possible. I have four for my pointers: *heel* (mostly so that I can confidently walk the dog back to my truck along a tarred road); *all right*, which sends the dog on; *whoa* and *dead* need no explanation, and after a brief spell, if I've been scrupulous and consistent, *whoa* drops out of the repertory.

Pete learned *heel*, as God will witness me, after about ten minutes on the check cord. *Whoa* was a bit longer in the learning, not in the yard but when I launched quail; it came with astonishing speed nonetheless, and has not needed a refresher since. *All right* was of course a snap. Because pointers are not famous for their retrieving skills, I didn't insist on a fetch back to hand: *dead* only meant I needed him to locate whatever just got knocked down in the puckerbrush.

For my money, training a pointing dog is really a matter of respecting and refining the dog's instincts, and then getting the hell out of the way. As my friend John Hayes, a first-rate professional handler in our Northeast Kingdom, once put it to me, "Some guys pay me $2500 for training their bird dogs, but most of it should go into training *them*." Or, as the late Bill White of Grand Lake Stream, Maine, once advised me when I was green at this business, "Soon as you learn that your dog knows a whole lot on his own, you'll be ready to use him right."

Pete got so steady on planted quail that, even when he could actually see the dumb little things on the ground, he held, and it was gratifying that in actual woods, away from the tall grass meadow where I'd worked him on the quail, he made excellent finds and points on released pheasants, never mind the heat and dryness of August and September. But half-tame quail and pen-raised pheasants are one thing. Soon enough I'd be off on that annual hunting trip to Montana, Pete in tow—and wild birds are quite another proposition.

My oldest hunting buddy, Peter Woerner, and I began in the Bear Paw Mountains. Usually I put off the western trip until November, because the New England season for ruffed grouse, which will always be my favorite bird, is so short that I don't want to miss any of October. I'd gone west early in the season this year only because I hoped that the sharptail—not yet having been much hassled—would be a bit more cooperative than the ruffs, and more so than they'd be themselves later along, holding well enough that Pete could get his nose into them. And the shots would be over open country, not the split-second affairs that our dense local woods afford, if they afford any at all.

The sharpies' wing-bursts and squawks, and their occasional tendency like any grouse to change locations before flushing, confused my pointer some, but only for a forenoon. After lunch on that first day, we were lucky enough to find quite a few birds, sufficiently near to one another that there weren't many breaks in the action, but not tightly coveyed, multiple eyes and ears conspiring against us.

There was a stiff mountain wind that first afternoon. We hunted into it, and Pete soon had scent. He went on, bold as I wanted him to be, and in the ten or twenty seconds between his making game on the first afternoon grouse and the point, I swore I saw the metaphorical light bulb flash on. From that moment forward, whether he was into a single grouse or a mess of Hungarian partridge, he looked for the most part astonishingly like a seasoned dog.

I have hunted and fished for so many years now that what I do can bring out a jadedness in me. To fool a big brown trout, for instance, in later life feels more satisfying than thrilling. I gave up deer hunting more than a decade ago. It didn't mean enough to me anymore to compensate for the endless hours of scouting, stalking, sitting, gutting, dragging. I still hunt turkeys, but rather casually, unwilling to cruise for hours in pursuit of a gobble; either a tom responds to me from where I set up, or he doesn't, and I go home.

To this day, however, I have an electric response to a dog holding a wild bird. The flush and shot are secondary. And there Pete was, locked up on that sharptail, the prairie grass rippling around him, the air sweet as flowers. I did not say, "Behold a miracle" to myself, but I damned sure felt something to that effect.

Maybe my hunting, or rather my dog-handling life, for which I have sustained such enthusiasm, has qualities echoed by my writing life, for which I have sustained the same. Neither has anything to do, Lord knows, with money or reputation, at least not in my case. Rather, the seduction lies in that enlivening process of setting out in pursuit of what Yeats called the "click": a moment when all your ranging and false starts and backtracks and frustrations and experience and intuitive moves somehow flow together and you suddenly come right smack on what you've been looking for all this time.

That's a miracle too, a payoff for having invested what you have invested in your life.

But all this may be subject for another inquiry. What's more, there's frankly something in me that resists making allegory of my days afield, however much it tempts me to do so. What my dog and I and the game do together is *not* encoded; it's direct and unmediated, and that's a boon. It's what keeps those days so fresh and dear. So back, precisely, to the field.

Our next stop was a hardscrabble ranch up near the Saskatchewan border, whose population of smaller birds had diminished significantly over the ten years we had visited there, but whose pheasants were still numerous.

Now anyone who knows pheasants by way of some hunting preserve doesn't know pheasants at all. The wild variety, especially if they've heard a few rounds of gunfire, are nearly as smart as our ruffed grouse. Like them, wild roosters learn how to keep something—a creek bank's shoulder, a hedge of willows, a single cottonwood—between themselves and the gun. Flushed, shot at, and missed, they will fly a half-mile if need be. And of course they will run.

Oh, how they'll run.

I was uneasy about leaving the grouse and the Huns, just as Pete had more or less gotten the hang of them, and traveling on to a territory full of ringnecks. Those running tendencies, I believed, would baffle my pup all over again. He did take another forenoon to wise up; then he caught the knack of moving with the bird until he could pin it—if it was pinnable. Some pheasants, of course, just scamper plumb out of the countryside.

Anyone reading this may, like me, hate the article in the outdoor magazines that claims a dog can do everything but brush the author's teeth and fold his laundry, especially if that author takes credit for these virtues. I'd hate to sound like one of that type, so let me admit that my youngster, indisposed to any mistakes I can see right now, will scarcely be flawless. I've never owned nor seen a dog to fit that description. No,

Pete is simply a great prospect, and I suspect he'll keep getting better as I provide him with more and more exposure. He'll improve, that is, if I remember Bill White's counsel: he already has a lot of knowledge by way of genetics. I only need to get him into the cover, give him exposure, and let instinct take over.

What will Pete's foible or foibles be? The first Wes would bring a woodcock halfway to me, then drop it and roll on it. Sam was a model citizen until his second season, when, rather than retrieving as he had in the first, he got rough-mouthed. Well, I understate. The first bird of season two was a woodcock, and I got to Sam just as the bird's feet were disappearing down his gorge, as if he were snake and his prey frog. I had subsequently to train him to point dead, not retrieve at all. By *her* second season, Belle wouldn't pick up a woodcock at all. For all of that, these were good animals, and were so chiefly, yes, because of exposure.

Yet I underexposed Pete at the ranch.

On our second evening there, I got sick. Very sick. Back at home, my wife and two of our children had recently contracted giardia, a debilitating parasitic ailment, and I began to wonder if I had now gotten a delayed dose of the same. I didn't know how else to explain the retching that kept me up almost to dawn.

As it turned out, giardia was not the villain, and I still don't know what was. Certainly not the ranch owner's cooking or her water, which I had been eating and drinking for a decade, and of which my longtime partner, Peter, as good a friend as a man could want, had consumed no less than I on this trip.

I didn't feel much like eating for a while, but the most painful effects of the bug diminished considerably after that one nasty night. The sickness left me, however, with next to no energy. I could lash myself through a morning, intent as I was on filling Pete's mouth with feathers and keeping the human Pete company; but after each midday break I was done.

As I sit here today, I feel about as fine and fit as a man my age has any right to feel. Since Montana, I have spent a peaceful and productive week at my Maine cabin, each day getting Pete into a fair supply of ruffed grouse. Retired from teaching, I'm dreaming up a Midwestern trip for later in the year. It's as though that enervated few days at the ranch never happened.

I'm lucky enough to have had no serious or chronic medical problems, but like anyone else, I've had episodes of compromised health, from an occasional flu to a self-inflicted chain saw gash that required a hundred stitches and a hundred staples. In those times, unable to do the physical things that are my life's sustenance, I've felt my spirits sag, if I may euphemize. And whenever I recuperate, I give myself the same familiar lecture: Count your blessings; don't forget what it's like when they're suspended. Like anyone, alas, I soon forget my own admonition, sound as it doubtless is.

All of this makes me think that the events and reflections I've recorded up to this point are, for the most part, a bit *beside* the point. In several ways, though, I do partly owe whatever may be worth saving from them to the pointer I praise—and to my awareness of what my brother-in-law and others have been through in the past few years.

On our last day in Montana, I went afield after breakfast, which for me had consisted of an unbuttered slice of toast. I still felt queasy, and the weather was dispiriting: a stiff east wind full of drizzle, and a sufficiently warm temperature that the prior day's dusting of snow had started melting. The mud underfoot transformed itself to what locals call gumbo, clay so heavy that early homesteaders used it to construct their houses. With every step, the clot of earth on my boots fattened, and it wasn't long before I wore what looked like gumbo snowshoes.

I'd been tired even before I left the ranch house. Under these conditions, a single hour had me pretty well played out. It was less some vestige of foolish male pride than an urge to keep Pete's nose into game that kept me going just the same, though the pheasants had gotten skittish and scarce since our first few shoots.

But something wondrous ensued.

I needn't even close my eyes to see what I saw about an hour later. There's a certain low mesa about a mile north of the ranch, the creek running tight to it but with a ribbon of CRP grasses, perhaps fifty yards wide, flanking its eastern side. I stop and lean against a lone cottonwood in the middle of that field, as beat as beat knows how to be. My legs are anchored by fatigue and clay. Raindrops seep down the back of my neck. We haven't moved a bird, or at least none close enough to shoot at, let alone for Pete to point, in some time.

Still, a palpable wave of gratitude washes over my body and soul. I contemplate my young dog, bold white against the gray mesa and the tawny grass, quartering with so much energy and enthusiasm you'd think we'd been finding rooster after rooster.

I love the way a pointer moves, enough so that even when I'm shooting over someone's superb setter or Brittany, I feel something has been left out of the movie. That's neither indictment of nor condescension to other breeds; I've seen and even owned some real go-getters without an ounce of pointer blood in their systems. I'm talking only of a sort of spiritual energy that charges my psyche. Head up, chest mighty, sinews rippling throughout his frame, for me Pete seemed an embodiment of physical perfection. What drive. What agility. What bodily intelligence in his every gesture. To see all that was to feel that life was more than worth living.

Like Wes II and all his much-mourned predecessors, Pete will probably be gone before I go (though a late sexagenarian should govern his certainties). Meanwhile, if death is the mother of beauty, sickness seems to mother some blessings too.

Peter Woerner, my oldest hunting partner, and I with bird dog Pete and Montana sharptails and ringnecks.

Daybook, November

In the very middle of the day today, a muskrat—for some unfathomable reason—attempted to cross the common in the very middle of our village.

Three men kicked it to death.

Had they extinguished the little animal by way of trapping it in season, I mightn't feel as sick as I do, even if to bludgeon it to death with a boot may in actuality have been less harsh than letting it drown in a water set.

Trapping taxes my morality to begin with, though I trapped 'rats myself as a kid, and with gusto, in the little Pennsylvania brook that fed my uncle's pond and, unbeknownst to its owner, a brook that fed a neighbor's.

I wouldn't do so now, yet I remember the care with which I checked toggles and cocked tines, the fastidiousness with which I skinned the little orange animals, salted their hides, and tacked them hair-side-out onto shingles in the tool shed. I recall that a hired man had put up a poster there. It showed an exhausted Native American man sprawled before a tent, from which peeked an equally cartoonish but beautiful woman. Underneath the picture was the puzzling caption, "A Buck Well Spent."

Once my pelts were well cured, I'd load them into the basket of my fat-wheeled Schwinn and ride them to the trader a mile or so down Butler Pike, now the site of a Staples and a Domino's Pizza. These and other dispiriting franchises have spread like wildfire into countryside where I rode my ponies, tied off grain sacks on a combine—and, yes, trapped 'rats. Those who assail the cruelty of trapping might consider if it is ultimately more malign than such utter obliteration of habitat.

That time I remember is ages behind me. But nowadays I know some people—professional trappers—who live much farther north from that childhood haunt, men I truly admire, even love. And by virtue of their enterprise, they know things about the ways of nature that our Staples-and-Domino's culture is largely unaware of.

It's also true that, trappers under such attack and their numbers so dwindled, epidemic among the overpopulated furbearers is rampant—mange in the coyotes, distemper in the 'coons, tularemia in the beavers, Errington's Disease in those muskrats—not to mention nuisances to humans—plugged culverts, flooded roads, breached dams. None of this, however, was on my mind as I sat inside my truck, mutely regarding a plain act of savagery.

Because wasn't it that? Or were these men poachers in the old mode, poor enough that a single small hide might provide some help in getting their families by? Much as I may have wanted to think so, these thugs would have had to be more than merely poor; they'd have had to be morons to believe such a calculation made the slightest sense, especially in a day when, the domestic market having shrunk so, fur must be sent to satellites of the old Soviet Union, and—like every other resource, it can sometimes seem—to China.

I'm nauseated by the incident because I believe the three killed that animal for the mere sake of killing something. They were a more hideous version of the deer hunter who, luckless all day, turns his rifle on a curious fisher or a careless fox. The 'rat was a bright and glossy novelty, a wild water creature come upland onto the town green, to which the men's response was neither wonder nor delight nor even amusement but imbecile violence.

The picture of those assassins—none, fortunately, known to me—sticks in the mind many hours later, and I fear it will stick for a long, long time. In my mind I'll watch the trio kick the poor thing back and forth between them like a ball, now and then clumsily hopping to avoid its pathetic efforts at self-defense. They all laugh.

I'm a hunter. Am I then, despite myself, a spiritual relative of these louts? God save my soul if so.

I drove off, tires screaming, lest I find that they left that creature right there where it died in panic.

God Bless Hunting

This morning, I've been sitting with Joey, one of my dearest friends and a field partner for decades, in the Red Dog diner. It's 6:30 a.m. on an early December day in this small, west Kansas town. After it gets light enough, we two mean to look up the native bobwhite and pheasant.

God bless hunting anyhow.

Without which no Joey, Terry, Dave, Landy, Ray, Allie, Creston, to name somewhat fewer than there have been. And without which no Red Dog.

The place is about full—it doesn't take much—and the clients on a weekend are either hunters themselves, mostly for deer, or farmers. The substantial majority have reached a certain age, and each is male. On entering, a newcomer strolls directly to the coffee urn, fills his cup, and joins companions at a long formica table. All the men wear hats, most showing feed brand logos.

The minute one fellow takes a chair, several others say something to him. I'm too shotgun-deaf to hear much over the background buzz, but whatever a particular remark may be, it immediately occasions a salvo of good-natured, joshing laughter. You could cut the camaraderie in this tiny room with a disc harrow.

No doubt most of my salaried friends, were I to mention my trip to Kansas, would have something sardonic or contemptuous to say. "What on earth could take you *there*?" I almost hear the question, drenched in condescension, from people who, as they'd admit or even boast, have never been *there*, people, that is, who are as sentimental and orthodox about their ironies as they accuse these unmet citizens of being about their values, including their religion.

Irony-as-orthodoxy is an odd phenomenon, to be sure. And judgment without inspection, speaking of irony, constitutes the very narrow-mindedness these colleagues claim to despise. Without a moment's reflection, they'd apply the word *provincial* to men like the ones Joe and I see here in the Dog, suggesting that those men have limited knowledge of the world—by which in fact the ironists really mean the world they themselves inhabit. For the self-styled sophisticates, you see, bigotry and clannishness are vices ... unless you revile the right people, the ones who don't belong to *their* clan. Then they're okay.

Between the Red Dog party and the disdainful party, whose insularity, objectively speaking, is the greater? Whose politics are more cartoonish?

There's no reason, given my background, my elitist training, and yes, even my own politics, to imagine I'd be any different from the people I challenge here, were I not a hunter. Hunting has provided me entrée to those Kansans in the diner and others like them in a lot of other places. The Red Dog customers amicably converse among themselves, and with us, regarding things we all have our reasons to care about: crops, weather, habitat, game populations, threats to those populations, and so on. If it goes without saying that I'm not one of them, I'm still more or less easy with their language.

For all those sporadic bursts of laughter, there's a courtliness in the eatery that, not to be smarmy, warms me on this cold prairie day. The Kansans may appear more open-handed, less guarded than the country people of my upper New England, but I'd be shocked if, like them, they don't make the best sorts of friends, ones who value loyalty, who show up, often unbidden, when you're in a bind, who do the things that most liberals mostly just talk about: help their needy neighbors, visit the sick ones, care for children in need.

I say this in full awareness that generalities are odious, and that if I went often enough to the Red Dog, or anywhere else on earth, I'd surely find counter-examples.

But I know what I know.

I know Joey, for instance, as I know few other men. A Vermont farm boy by birth, he started his working life as a carpenter and turned into a very accomplished and successful builder. He put up a house for us in the last town we lived in, and the one in the town where we live now, and will, I hope, for the rest of our lives. These are excellent houses. I knew they'd be that because, from the time he was a mere kid, Joey and I have shared so many outings looking for game.

People who know what I mean will know what I mean.

I have had the opportunity to associate with good people like this best of companions, and again, that's because I'm a hunter, by which I mean a real hunter, a claim that does not in turn mean I'm a particularly good shot (I'm streaky is what I am, sometimes hot, others stone cold), nor that my sense of where the game hides transcends the norm, nor that my way with sign or cover or dogs is better than the next person's. Whether I possess such gifts or not is secondary anyway. When I use the descriptive "real," I suggest only that I want my quarry wild, not farm-raised and plunked in some preserve; that I intend the hunt to be managed by me and/or one or more of these friends, not served up by some hiree; that I believe in working for my prey, having striven lifelong to develop the capacities that can lead me toward it.

Above all, it means that whatever company I keep will see the day's hunt the way I do: as the only mission worth thinking about for the time being. I don't want to stop and talk about political affairs, books, personalities, and so on.

In this way I may distinguish myself, I'd argue, from those few of my economic class or educational background who call themselves hunters in the first place, and who are in fact shooters. I'll concede that many of them are damned good shooters, several better than I, but they are a different breed of outdoorsman, to call them so. (I'd meant to avoid *ad hominem* reference to such self-described hunters as Antonin Scalia and the attorney-strafing Dick Cheney, but weakness of will prevails.)

I would never have had the advantages for which I am so grateful if I had been that sort of sport. And this morning, I reflect that one such advantage is represented by the tatterdemalion and distinctly non-gourmet Red Dog Diner. I've savored the old grease in which my bacon and eggs were cooked. I've relished the wildlife art on the walls, which is not good, precisely; rather, it precisely chimes with the setting, which somehow seems more important.

And the chatter here is pure music:

You leavin', Will? asks a beefy guy in bib overalls.

Yep.

Now there's a blessin'! teases the fallen-arched, thin-haired older woman, owner and waitress both.

His buddies cackle.

We're leaving too. Joey holds the door for a gent named Jack, who inquires how our luck has been. We allow that we haven't been finding many birds, don't know the country well enough, and may not get time to figure things out, given the mere five days we've set aside.

"No one's hunted my milo patch yet," Will muses, "and I cut 'er late." He invites us to follow him.

We thank Jack and hop into Joey's truck, imagining the edges of that field holding quail, and, wide of them, tall grass full of ringnecks. As we trail along, the sun breaches the eastern horizon, revealing the opalescent frost on everything we behold. By God, this part of Kansas is pretty, I think, another notion the aprioristic judges on either coast would likely never surmise. A wonderful terra cotta shade displays itself in the prairie grass; the forbidding plum thickets might have been wrought by a woodcutter's burin; the milo stubble shows reddish, the corn stubble spectral. Through his rear window, I note the deep crosshatching in Jack's weathered neck. It's good to be alive.

I'm pretty sure Jack thinks so too. Something about the way he sits, half-turned on his seat, taking in views that must be as familiar to him as his wife or his children, but perhaps strike him afresh every day.

I know the feeling.

I know as well that it's too tempting and too glib to take this line of thought very far. Generalities *are* odious, and there may be, nay likely is, as much neurosis and pettiness and inexplicable emotional pain among the folks in this neighborhood as among any. Still there's something salutary, I insist, about being attuned to seasonal and physical attributes of the natural world, something I get, of course, not as a farmer but as a hunter, who, whatever the time of year, finds himself in constant study of the countryside.

The more "virtual" and disembodied and addicted to gadgetry our world becomes, the more valuable such direct engagement. Or so I believe in any case, even if I may be cataloguing beliefs that sustain *me* and applying them to other people, whether they're true sustenance for them or not. My mind slips off to my own wife and children. I wonder if the game dinners

I've served them have meant nearly as much to them as to me, for example. I've always felt some profound rightness in such meals, as if the world's symmetries were ingestible by the ones I cherish too. I know exactly where that flesh we eat has come from, and I relive my time there as we gather at the table.

But I can only make my own testimony, which has its gaps, I concede. Thanks to the miracle of the very modern technology I mildly slurred a moment ago, before Joe and I walked into the Red Dog I received a photograph from my son-in-law in Brooklyn. It came by cellular phone, for the love of God. It showed his and my daughter's ten-month-old mixed-race twins; to open it up was to feel a positive surge of affection.

Which raises the question: how, Mr. Real Hunter, do you construe a continuum between the world that these babies will learn and the world of the Red Dog, of Jack and his cronies, between the glowing milo patch and the Midwood section of Brooklyn? Or, to think randomly of some other thing that heartens me, how to link my abiding passion, honed in college years spent near New York, for certain legends of jazz—Thelonious Monk, Miles Davis, Bill Evans, Max Roach, on and on—to this warm feeling in the cab of a pickup as we trail some sweet old redneck to his dirt farm?

When I dreamed up this series of essays, I imagined that in one of them at least I'd wrestle these antinomies into harmony. But I need to face it: I just can't. It seems I know enough of urbane sophistications, no matter my suspicions of them, *and* of rural concerns that I'll never cleave to one exclusively of the other.

I'd be tempted to justify myself by quoting Walt Whitman on self-contradiction: *I am large, I contain multitudes.* I might do so, that is, if I didn't believe this to be true of anyone, or if I didn't believe too that my own are modest enough. Lord knows I'm anything but large in any case, at least spiritually. There are times, I confess, when the sense of my radical limitations makes me ponder whether my attraction to the allegedly simple life is not a sort of retreat.

I'm not the one to answer that. If retreat it be, though, I'm too old in it. Not enough years remain for me to undo these addictions and affections, even if I live to a ripe age. Not that I yearn to undo them, not at all, because I do feel affection and something much deeper than that for the life I've chosen, conflicted though it sometimes may seem.

Nor is it unthreatened. I've now dwelt forty-four years in upper New England. Rampant gentrification has twice pushed me northerly, the town I first lived in so demographically changed that it's plain unrecognizable to my eyes, and the next rapidly following suit. In the late 1960s I knew all but a very few local families in my town. I'm acquainted with next to none there these days.

Houses belonging to a single family line through five generations are either gone or enormously altered. The ones that stand, once fortified against winter by hay bales at the sills, are now remodeled so thoroughly that they'd settle perfectly into Fairfield County, Connecticut. Dooryards that in mud-time saw hens and roosters parading over mired ruts are manicured in 2012. Trees from which, come November, slain bucks hung are now trimmed and skirted by perennials bought from self-described heritage seed purveyors. Fields of fallen farms, grown up in aspen and hardhack and gray birch, have been brush-hogged, tilled, and sown with fescue, eliminating acres of habitat for wildlife, which new residents, innocent of the wild things' ways, think they protect by tacking up their *No Hunting* posters. All these are the perplexing signs made by people concerned to transform what they fled to into what they lately fled *from*.

Not of course that I recall an idyll, except perhaps for me. For more than two centuries, it was more than merely hard for families to scratch livings out of that quarter; those deserted farmlands would not have been so game-rich, would not have gone to brush and joe-pye weed if it had been otherwise. And there were soreheads and backbiters and cheats among the north country natives. I knew them too. Still, I believe that "people neighbored better then," as one of the last from the old families lately put it to me. In my memory at least, the lunch counter at the hardware store rang with the buzz we'd just left behind at the Red Dog.

In those early years, I was among the slight minority of college-educated people in that hamlet. Members of this group tended to know one another, but if they knew a native, it was because he or she provided a service: car repair, plowing, carpentry, bread-making, child care, whatever. Hunting, and to a lesser degree fishing, provided me with another access to these famously terse and even suspicious people. Not that there were no alternate ways to bond with them. For instance, I have a close friend who, though a distinguished architect in later life, did a lot of hammer-swinging when he started, thereby gaining local respect. But hunting was my way.

And perhaps the main point of these meditations is this: I forged ties, very alive today, whether in fact or in my recollections of the departed, to people who have proved to be friends like no others.

I recall, say, standing stock-still one morning at the edge of the swamp near Trout Pond with the late Allie Pike, our road commissioner. The snow floated down, backlit by sun over Smart's Mountain. Allie's beagle and my own were running on scent, his Stony ball-mouthed, my Penny a chop. I can't remember whether we shot the hare they were ragging, but I remember feeling as though this tangle of alder, this bottomland of fresh snow, and this ten-degree day all constituted some quasi-Arctic Eden. I have, and always will have, that moment to refer to.

Back then, though in my better self I already knew as much, I learned that there were people who had never heard of Harvard or Princeton, and who were bright, even brilliant. And that is exactly what such places— whatever their PR folks and parlor-leftie faculties may claim—teach their students *not* to believe. At freshman convocation at Yale, the president greeted me and my classmates as "future leaders of the world," which could only mean that most of the people outside the hall were there to be led.

In short, one learns not only a certain attitude but also a certain encoded language at the so-called top-tier schools, and one must not so much unlearn that idiom as learn or relearn others if one wants a richer mix in life.

Hunting pervades every aspect of that life for me. Back when I decided I was more drawn to imaginative writing than to scholarship, for instance, it was the voices of my hunting mentors and their female partners that drove me primarily to poetry. I knew that I didn't have the genius of a Mark Twain or a Flannery O'Connor, or that I couldn't hope to celebrate the speech of upper New England by writing dialect, so damnably hard to construct without either condescension or embarrassing affectation. For better or worse, I thought that if I chose a poetic vehicle, I might capture the rhythms and cadences of local speech without having to *imitate* it.

Some of my local hunting friends have read my work in prose, but not many—indeed none, I surmise—have mounted anything like an exhaustive inspection of my poems. And yet, whenever I compose a lyric or, especially, a verse narrative, I imagine myself as addressing one or all of them. That is, I know, just an enabling strategy; it makes no earthly sense at all.

Small wonder I literally wept when Joey, the fellow beside me as we follow Jack's pickup out to this section land, decided a decade ago that he too would move ahead of "progress." But he chose Colorado, land of the mule deer and bull elk, for his refuge. Small wonder I've laughed with joy and amusement to catch up with him again here in Kansas, and why laughter has leavened the seriousness of our enterprise since we started the trip. Because of our collaborations, now and over countless days, I am as sure as I am writing this that, if I called out to Joey in some dire need, he'd be on a plane from Denver within a day. And I'd fly the other way for him in a heartbeat.

Joey has always called me Professor Woodcock, though we both quit shooting those little flyers years ago, dismayed by the great falling off of their numbers—who'd have guessed?—since the days when we'd kill more than a hundred in a season. Along with his Yankee peers, he's also always called my academic colleagues *pinheads.*

Something he said back at the Red Dog was right on the money, and right in keeping with what I'm after here: "The pinheads don't have no idea a scene like this exists, Professor Woodcock."

The concrete meaning of the pinhead epithet, if there is just one, as there doubtless is not, may remain obscure, but as a general notion it's clear. A pin is a small thing. Though angels may dance upon it, it is not large enough to contain Whitman's human multitudes, or any. I've confessed to containing only modest ones myself, but I do hope I'm not a pinhead, or at least not only that. I pray my human purview is not so severely confined.

If that's the case, then yes, God bless hunting anyhow. Again. And again.

Jack pulls into his farmyard. A sun-flaring ginger rooster, late to greet the forenoon, chants from a crippled weathervane on top of the barn. We all get down from our vehicles.

"Just walk past my silo to the other end. You'll want to hunt upwind," Jack advises.

Joey and I shake our benefactor's hand before he disappears into his corrugated tractor shed. We set out in the direction the farmer just indicated.

Twenty yards along the border of the milo piece, Joey commented, "That old boy's paw feels like braided cable."

Joey Olsen, builder extraordinaire and longtime beloved companion.

Daybook, December

I imagine taking another person to this corner of our home place, speaking of its restorative power, watching him or her frown in confusion. My companion beholds the four hop hornbeams, no thicker than forearms, that cling to a scrap of ledge on the west, looks at the clump of paltry hemlocks to eastward, at a depression to the north quilled with equally paltry cedar.

I've never encountered any remarkable game in this fifty-yard square, nor fall-splendid foliage, nor tinkling spring freshets, deep summer cool, fabulously sculpted ice on the granite shelves. But there's a sort of rock-seat there. Once I perch on it, as I do by habit, I always feel something regenerative blow into my soul like a real breeze. A cure for the blues, you could say, which has nothing to do with poetry, my stock in trade. I observe none of my region's tokens of human effort nullified: no stone wall spilling itself to rubble; no woodpile abandoned to shimmer in its moldering; no apple tree pocked by woodpeckers.

I've now and then tried to make sense of this ground's hold on me. Of course the place belongs to us, not in the sense that our family owns it except by law, but that no other creature seems its familiar. Even deer prints are anomalies; I'd see none, I bet, in this morning's fresh snow if I went out; the ground offers no cover for game bird or hare; but the place's exclusivity to all but me can't be a full explanation of its attraction either.

Is it the quiet? Is it that I can be alone here with my silent thoughts, which are, in general, hardly thoughts at all? I don't sleep on my rock-seat but I'm not mentally active, either. A floret from one of the hornbeams may fall beside me, for instance, and I make nothing of it.

But I don't really believe the place's silence, apart from a wind now and then, explains its effect on me any more than our proprietorship does.

There's simply some energy in this patch of landscape that I can marshal against my grief over the death of relative or friend or bird dog; against some professional setback; against excruciations large and little. The nature of that energy is inscrutable. And I believe that its very indefiniteness (I some-times "see" it, but only as one sees squiggles of heat off stone on a hot day) lies at the heart of its magic.

Natural magic, you may rightly say, is everywhere. We must do all we can to protect it in the contiguous great north woods; we must struggle against the cupidity and shortsighted-ness that would introduce nickel mines to the great Labrador wild, hew the rain forests of Brazil, strip the tops from West Virginia mountains, pollute the world's clear lakes, extinguish its wildlife.

But it occurs to me that we should do all this in part because those sublime domains include inconspicuous places like this one, which will never show on calendar or travel brochure. These are the places whose aura defies the simplistic slogans of the environmental absolutist, of the exploiter drunk on his own greed, and even of the solitary eccentric who breathes that magic in.

I guess I'll head to such a place right now.

Trust

"That's Annie's camp," I told my wife.

The little structure showed vaguely through the softwood. Beyond it, Lower Oxbrook Lake barely winked in the overcast October forenoon. The scene jolted me into the sort of recognition I've been having so often lately: Lord, I hadn't set foot on that ground since Annie Fitch and her husband Bill were much younger than I right now.

Robin and I had just hiked down and back along the redundantly named Oxbrook Brook, from the stream's mouth on West Grand Lake to where we stood now, a pretty jaunt but not vigorous. We weren't tired and were in no hurry.

"Let's go look," Robin urged, a not quite familiar expression on her face.

Closer to, I saw that the building and the camp yard had changed some. After Bill died, Annie passed the property on to her daughter Ginnie, whose husband Vinny had been a master electrician before he retired, working at the pulp mill in Woodland. But he was equally handy in every other way that went into construction and maintenance, so there wasn't a hair out of place anywhere you looked. The camp's roof was in good order, all the siding recently stained, the doors plumb. Shading our eyes and peering through a back window, we even saw a washing machine! It drew its water in summertime from Oxbrook's cool depths, a generator in the shed providing the juice. The old privy was gone.

The place looked a lot more comfortable in outward and visible ways, but I remembered another sort of comfort here. I could almost smell the trout we'd caught not far from the dock, wild squaretails sizzling in fat on a wood-fired cook-stove. At the same time, Annie was turning a mess of white perch, yanked from a different honey-hole across the water, into her glorious chowder.

We peeked through as many other windows as we could. Sleeping loft, tiny master bedroom, "settin' room," kitchen. That was about it. The place was locked, as it wouldn't have been in the Fitches' time. Some changes are good, others ambiguous.

Bill and his father Harley had put up the original cabin in 1961, a base for their market fur line, which followed the stream to the cove, as we'd just done. Harley had another, even more modest encampment down there on the lake. Either man could repair to either cabin, whichever was handier when he finished a day of checking and resetting traps.

In my mind, this muted sunlight glinted off Harley's wire-rimmed glasses. I could see that stubby pipe clenched between his teeth, as if it might fly away if he didn't keep it clamped in. And I remembered Bill even better, as clearly as if I'd greeted him that very morning. Lean, even slight, he was unprepossessing to the eye, but Annie recalled his walking to and fro on the timber road, hugging a hundred-pound cement bag like a baby every trip down to the cabin site, more than a mile. He was a famous strongman in his younger years, a finger-crimper of silver dollars, a bender of ten-penny nails, a hefter of nail kegs. And understated? As one of his cronies put it, "Bill was drier'n a popcorn fart."

I was once hunting whitetail out in the Getchel Pugs country. I came upon Bill and his party, a man I'll call Dr. Miles and his wife. A couple days before at the store, Bill had told me they were due, and he didn't seem to be looking forward particularly. He had guided these two for twenty years, and they were nice enough, all right, but they had the somewhat endearing and somewhat otherwise habit of moving off the stands at which Bill placed them and coming together to chat. That may have made for marital harmony, but not good deer strategy.

Bill and his clients were seated on a flat rock, eating sandwiches and waiting for the camp coffee to boil over the fire. I asked if they minded my joining them. There was plenty of room on that boulder, and they welcomed me.

Now Dr. Miles and his wife were fitted out with top-of-the-line equipment, from their suspiciously untattered Abercrombie clothing to their rifles. He was sporting a Weatherby Mark V, a relatively new piece in the early '60s, I think.

I had the same inherited deer rifle I'd always used and always would: a Winchester .32-.20 WCF, and Bill toted its more famous cousin, the .32 special. For whatever reason, Bill volunteered that he'd recently gotten interested in a Rueger .44 mag, and I informed him that a pal of mine was mightily pleased with his. The comment wasn't even true, but I liked being on Bill's side of things.

Our remarks set the good doctor off on a rant for some reason. "I wouldn't buy a Rueger *anything*," he spat. "Their rifles are worthless, their side arms too. Same for their shotguns!"

He proceeded to catalog all the defects of this line of weaponry, and never mind the fact that, Mark V or no, he had not even shot *at* a deer in two decades of hunting here. Bill had told me that too.

When Dr. Miles finally ran down, Bill looked bemusedly into the horizon, as was his manner, and whispered, "Well, ain't no use in buyin' one of them, then."

One of my sisters still refers to Bill's wife Annie as The Good Mother, a distinction I'm disinclined to dwell on in these pages. But all of us siblings regarded Annie that way, as did everyone in her little hamlet. People admired her competence, as much as they did her famous cooking; she served for years as the town treasurer, was a mainstay of its tiny Congregational church, and played counselor to those who needed help with all manner of problems.

This great woman spent the better part of our summer stay as a guest at our island camp after she retired, and so went on to become The Good Grandmother to my generation's offspring too. I'm beyond sorry that she didn't get to know our children's children, but that they didn't get to know *her* constitutes the greater sadness. They also, like our kids, would always have referred to the place as Annie's Island. She was someone you'd name things after, that's all; she was bigger than whatever she inhabited.

Rising early, she'd come into the cookhouse, carrying this or that romance novel, which she plowed through at a pace to embarrass a professional reader like me. Ordinarily the first out of bed, I'd have her usual odd breakfast waiting: a cup of hot water and a dry waffle.

Seated a few feet from the woodstove in the rocker that came, of course, to be called Annie's Chair, she would talk all day to whomever, not in some garrulous way, but filling her listeners in, the stories inexhaustible, on what life had been like for her and her neighbors from the time of her girlhood into middle age—which meant, to put it gently, hard.

Yet, as I said at an earlier point in these musings, she claimed to have savored every particle. "I don't have one thing to complain about." How many times did I hear those words pass Annie Fitch's lips?

I remember coming on a grade school picture that the prior owners, decades and decades before, had stashed away in the back of a cupboard. It wasn't a photograph of Annie's class, but of one or two before hers. Still she picked out every face, identified it, and went on to recount what had happened to each person she named. A very few were still in town, far more were dead, and a handful, some living, most gone, had spread out as far as western Canada. She was in touch with those still reachable; the lady had a great gift for loyalty.

After supper, Annie joined our family and friends in games, anything from cribbage, at which I never saw her lose, to the smallest child's favorites: Candyland, Chutes and Ladders, and others. Nothing was beneath her, and nothing much above. It might have surprised a stranger that she did so well at Trivial Pursuit, for example, this backwoods-woman who'd worked her way through high school down in Calais, housekeeping for a doctor and his wife, tending to their children, who, if any endures, surely remember The Good Mother too, or rather The Good Big Sister.

Her store of knowledge might have surprised us as well if we hadn't learned early on never to be taken aback by any prowess Annie showed. She was one whose eyes stayed wide open right through her last year, the ninetieth, with never any doddering or mental vagueness, and with that razor memory, so keen that people, neighbors and vacation folks alike, automatically consulted her whenever some issue of town history came up. I wouldn't be able to count how often I did so myself.

When her husband died, we all feared that Annie might go into a tailspin. She and Bill had always sat like teenagers in their pickup truck as they cruised the few passable roads, the only difference being that she always had the wheel. Bill must have wanted her in charge. Most people did.

Annie Fitch was a big, raw-boned lady, though not a fat one, tough as nails when she had to be. My daughters made her tell one short anecdote every summer, never failing to delight in it.

"There was this boy down to the high school who had a fancy for me, but I wasn't interested," she'd begin, her lip curling in an altogether uncharacteristic sneer.

"One day when we were all headed out to go home, he come right up behind and tickled me. Well, I didn't like that, and I just saw red. I turned and gave him a punch, put him right over the rail of the schoolhouse.

"He got up and said, 'Hey, I was only foolin'.' I just told him, 'Well, I *wasn't!*' "

So here we stood, at Annie's Camp, as it too will always be known. A FOR SALE sign was staked at the head of the dooryard path. Ginnie and Vinny had recently built a new house on the shore of Big Lake, toward Princeton, and they spent a fair portion of the winters in Florida now anyhow. I knew they'd been trying to unload the Oxbrook property, but the real estate swoon begun in 2007 had left it without a buyer for these three years.

"Are you thinking what I think you're thinking?" my wife asked.

"And you are too," I replied. It might make sense. It really might make sense.

My brother and sisters and I took over the management of my parents' island after our mother's death in 2000. We had children of our own, and some already had children themselves. It was going to be increasingly complicated to sort out which crowd would be there, and when. If we had Annie's Camp, our own direct line would have something that was theirs alone in this dear territory.

Of course I already owned my beloved river camp in the village, and had lately refurbished it, if not quite so elaborately perhaps as Vinny might have. Was I bidding to become a local land baron? No, but our grandchildren would be imperiled by the crashing rapids of Big Falls, the way their own parents had been when they were small. As all this progeny burgeoned, there'd be more than one option for my descendants if there was a full house at the bigger family place.

That was the objective rationale. The deeper one had to do with some sense of symmetry in our taking possession of our priceless friend's retreat. It somehow felt as though to own Annie's Camp would almost be to enter her very bloodstream, to feel her generous spirit coursing through us until we too were gone. Then it would flow through our grandchildren; they hadn't known Annie, but they would somehow know her in their futures.

Robin and I believed this instinctively. Annie was a haunt, benign as one could ever be.

Now Vinny and Ginnie were the last people on earth we wanted to take advantage of, but we did know their price had sunk over time, despite their having bought out the lease on the camp property so that the plot would be freehold. To the eventual delight of our bankers, we made our decision on the spot.

There was, however, yet another motive. That camp would in due course be engulfed, or so we profoundly hoped and still do, by a sustainable 22,000-acre community forest, one dedicated to the people of the settlement, perpetuating perhaps above all the traditional uses—hunting, fishing, canoeing, trapping, and so on—they had practiced for 180 years, clients in tow or not. I'm the chair of the campaign for those acres, which the local land trust means to acquire in three phases: first, the development rights to half, then those of the other half, and ultimately, all being as it should, the trust will buy the acreage outright.

The trust's brochure explains that the current effort "will protect the key 21,700-acre gap in a nearly 1.4 million-acre international wildlife corridor between Maine and New Brunswick. This is a big hurdle in a successful effort to conserve the Downeast Lakes and over 370,000 acres of forests."

1.4 million acres, a mass of land and water that's larger than my home state of Vermont—the notion will thrill me forever.

The project includes the eastern shoreline of West Grand Lake and eastward still through largely coniferous woods to Big Musquash Stream, one of the loveliest and most unspoiled wetlands in North America. On the far side of Musquash lies Passamaquoddy land, and the tribe has wholeheartedly supported our efforts from early on, two chiefs in a row serving as campaign members.

The West Grand Lake Community Forest will be managed in accord with the Forestry Stewardship Council's "green" guidelines. It will be managed, too, as much for wildlife as for timber, with the wildlife's habitats in fact getting preference at any point when the two might come into conflict. In these respects, it will be like 34,000 acres of woods on the other shore of West Grand, the Farm Cove Community Forest, which was part of a vaster project, grassroots at its very heart, for which my brother Jake and I and many others had also labored long and hard during the first ten years of the century. The land trust—in partnership with the New England Forestry Foundation—had succeeded in completing the Downeast Lakes Forestry Partnership, which involved the purchase of that Farm Cove territory, together with the development rights to over 300,000 further acres.

All along, I must confess, I longed for a time when the very need to do this work, to preserve the wildness of this neighborhood, would have been the last thing on anyone's mind. For well over a century, locals in this region were in many ways beyond the reach of what others called the modern world, and most were content to be. If they left for employment elsewhere, almost all made their ways back.

I'd lived in that blithe period, the end of it, as it turned out, and I had loved it. That was then, however, and this is now. I've had to face up to the fact. So have a lot of folks.

The work goes forward. Those of us who are deeply committed to it were of course delighted when, in 2010, our project was selected by the federal Forest Legacy Council as the number one forestry conservation project in the United States. As such, it stood to receive a crucial $6,700,000 in aid toward its completion. We could also expect a million via the North American Wetlands Conservation Act, or NAWCA.

In 2011, however, the new House majority in Washington recommended that these grants either be zero-funded or radically diminished. Of course, close as I've been to this effort, I was bound to grumble at such a decision, especially given the majority's unwillingness to consider wastefulness, say, in the military.

Yet I won't let what started in tenderness turn even briefly to mere polemic. The money did come through, after all, thanks in considerable measure to the advocacy of Maine Senator Susan Collins. I believe that she, like so many of us closely involved in this endeavor, saw our project as something beyond mere tree-hugging. In this dirt-poor corner of the nation, even to work on a crew that installs and maintains culverts for the hauling roads is a boon. Old-time employment in actual logging and related operations is rarer and rarer in the Northeast—as in a lot of America now, the pulp and paper industry having first gone literally south, to places like Arkansas and Alabama and Mississippi, where environmental laws and labor costs were less restrictive than in the north country, and then overseas, thanks to the marvels of globalization, to Poland, Slovakia, Siberia, and, of course, China.

So no, no rant from me, whose most genuine motive for involvement had been Harley, Annie, Bill, and many like them, people who have meant so much to me for as long as I've lived. Sustainable forestry, the harvesting of specialty wood, species-focused cutting, that is, would have a much weaker hold on my imagination if all didn't have these crucial human applications.

The word *ecology*, after all, is based on a Greek root meaning *home*; the traditional uses that our effort means to guarantee, then, have as much to do with the homeland, the community, of men and women and children as with that of beaver, fisher, moose, salmon, and rare black tern, profoundly important as all these doubtless are.

Our effort means to safeguard and promote the economic activity to which guides—our area having the greatest number in the state of Maine—can point, along with lodge owners. Forest practices that keep the woods *and* the wildlife, aquatic and terrestrial, in good health are essential in this respect too. Had the effort been aimed at the mere setting aside of wilderness for the pleasure of those who like us could afford to visit it, Jake and I might not have signed on.

After my wife and I made our decision, our friend Dave Tobey told us he was glad we'd decided to buy the place. Like me, like Robin, he thought this marked a proper line of descent. I'm proud that he thinks so, though no matter how much a woodsman I half-rightly think myself, given yet another seven decades I'd be no Harley, let alone Dave.

Dave is one of the most intelligent and canny people in my circle, a guide and hunter and trapper of exorbitant intellectual and natural curiosity, more so than even Harley or Bill. He was crucial to the founding of the land trust; he and several other local guides charted a course of action when word got out that their neighborhood was up for liquidation logging and development.

"If that happens, then you can kiss our way of life goodbye," they told one another.

And surely he was right. Either that whole mass of forest land, including the entire west shore of beautiful West Grand, would go the way of a Lake Winnepesaukee in New Hampshire, or some of that state's Upper Connecticut Lakes, quarter-acre lots dotting the shores, or worse, so far as the locals were concerned, it would be transformed into a few "kingdom estates," complete with chains and bars and *No Trespassing* signs.

That corner of Maine owes Dave and the others a vote of thanks. I'm not embarrassed to call them heroes.

"Too bad," Dave commented, "you couldn't buy the stories along with the camp."

Amen.

And yet I do know a few of those stories by way of Harley himself, his son, and especially, as I've indicated, his daughter-in-law. There's the one about Paul Hoar, the village storekeeper, for example, who remained handsome as Apollo until he died in his mid-nineties.

One year, shortly after the Second World War, Paul was guiding a female deer hunter out in that section, and Harley guiding one of her friends. It seems there came a dreadful early-evening snowfall, a virtual whiteout, and Harley rightly advised his sportswoman that they'd do best to head for the lakeshore camp.

Paul and his client did make it back to Paul's truck, and he understood not to wait around. Harley knew that territory out by Lower Oxbrook well enough to negotiate it blindfolded. He'd be all right. Paul would drive back and fetch him and his sport come dawn.

Next morning, Annie told me, the whole party reunited at Weatherby's Lodge, where she was cooking, and where the women hunters had taken a room for the trip.

"Where were you last night?" inquired Paul's client.

"We stayed out to Harley's camp," the other replied.

"Damn!" said her friend, a word rarely heard from genteel ladies in those days. "*Damn!* I've been trying to get stranded with *my* guide all week long!"

Annie remembered Paul blushing and excusing himself to "go check to see the ammunition weren't wet." Even the Boston ladies must have known the silliness of such an alibi.

That was the yarn that came to me as Robin and I stood on the stoop of Annie's Camp. I chuckled aloud.

"What's funny?" she asked.

"I'll tell you when we live here," I answered.

We walked down to the lake, where a familiar feeling crept into my being. Gazing at the unspoiled far shore, with its pickets of driftwood and its lichen-fuzzed stone, I suddenly remembered a bass fishing trip with my brother after the Downeast Lakes project had been completed.

For the preceding decade, Jake and I had been deep in thought about conserving that great swath. We were in and out of meetings, making phone calls one after the other, traveling to push for donations. Thus preoccupied, we'd almost forgotten the bigger picture. Remarkably, or not so remarkably perhaps, we both looked up at the same time on another back lake, scanning its beautiful ridges and shoreline. We thought out loud, "This will never change!"

I won't speak for Jake, though I bet I could. In that moment I recognized that our parts in effecting this result, though we were a mere two of many, needless to say, would likely be the most important ones we'd ever play, at least as citizens, in our earthly spans.

The wind suddenly picked up on Lower Oxbrook Lake as my wife and I made ready to leave. I noticed a brilliantly white gull fighting against it, aiming at Grand Lake, but soon, it would seem, thinking better; it banked abruptly, then soared right toward us where we stood, a few feet from water's edge. Now the bird turned again, hovering just overhead, almost motionless, the stiff blow suspending it. We could nearly have touched it.

In that instant, I remembered an account passed down by her father Frank MacArthur to the place's prior owner, Good Mother Annie. After the death of his wife Nelly, her own good mother, Frank was out in his canoe, glum, bait-fishing for his lonely dinner. Suddenly, just such a gull dropped onto his bow.

"I know it was Nellie," Frank told his daughter. "She said she'd come back to look after us, and she'd be a white bird."

I am neither a mystic nor given to superstition, but I think back on that moment as I write this, when the bright gull hung like a lantern at the Oxbrook camp, and I somehow feel trust. I'm sure that Annie and others like her will hover over our struggles, will see to it that we conserve as much as possible, human and wild, public and personal, of what we've come over decades to love.

Photograph by Steve Takach

Bill Fitch, co-builder of the Oxbrook camp and Annie's life companion, tonging out ice.

Cold Time: Reprise

Daybook, January

I took a hike to The Lookout yesterday, a day that soon became my latest candidate for Most Beautiful of Winter. Now words must fail to render it.

They'll fail to render you, too, Mt. Moosilauke, accursed and blessed! As the air of late afternoon purged itself for one of those nights of severe, absolute clarity, you took on a glow like caramel; today you show a lilac, to give some puny name to a color ineffable, beyond the capacities of the great watercolorists.

From now on, I shouldn't try to describe the mountain, or this feeling of bittersweet frustration that she spawns in me. I should work at some oblique remove from her. Having been cleansed by the mountain's grandeur—for good, I always think—I can make myself ready for other, lesser responses to other, lesser things.

So, to start again as easily as possible, the day was indeed beautiful, as always in this month, provided we have adequate light. I sometimes wonder, in fact, how it is that people so revile this month; the response seems automatic, not thought through. Surely I can't be the only watcher to have witnessed a yesterday so splendid, to have known such glorious January light.

The morning had broken gray, the world reduced to grim flatness, flat grimness. But that was a necessary lull. Out of it, given sunshine, everything could erupt again into the sort of splendor I find more moving than autumn's. It seems to cause an actual ache, too much of which would destroy me.

I had an absurd and absurdly grandiose thought on wandering downhill from The Lookout: the north country, I mused, may be a bit like me. Not of course with regard to beauty, but rather to something like temperament. Those given to astrology could provide an explanation, itself of course absurd and grandiose: I'm a Capricorn, thus tending to reserve, resistant to highfalutin' notions of the sublime. Since I'm born on the

Sagittarian cusp, however, one might predict occasional airiness, artiness, hyperbole from me.

Needless to say, I disbelieve entirely in such foolishness. If I'm a border character, that was a geographical matter at most in the moment I describe. I'd been standing on a granite hill, almost as far east as you can go in Vermont, gazing across the river at a much vaster one in New Hampshire, nearly as far west as you can get in that state.

Who needs to go beyond such mere facts? And yet on a day like yesterday, just as that glory of land and air could burst from drabness, so indeed may I break out of suspicion and skepticism, at least temporarily, leaping into romance.

Bring on the elves and fairies.

Wild Black Duck

I am reducing a sauce whose recipe came down to me, like so many, from Annie Fitch. I hear it bubbling over the stove's low heat; soon it will look a little like maple syrup, and in due course it will complement the wild black duck that my wife and I will be sharing this evening, New Year's Eve, which will find us in bed before the famous ball drops way south, in the city.

I will grill the bird over oak coals in an outdoor hearth. I mean, how else would anyone cook it?

I lost my brilliant duck dog Topper some nineteen years ago, and have hunted few ducks since. I made such a drastic training mistake on his successor Rosie (I'm embarrassed to go into detail) that she, or rather I, washed out. Muddy, the bitch pup who was meant to be her successor, turned out to have so many major health problems—a pair of intestinal surgeries before she was even two—that I could never train her, and there hasn't been an apt moment since to find another duck dog, three dogs already in our house quite enough.

But Topper's death by cancer (a more and more common story among dogs in our time, especially purebreds) coincided with other discouragements. I used to wait until the second half of our season for the ducks, the whole month of October given to ruffed grouse over pointing dogs. But November and December ducks here have always been the migratory blacks, the red-legged ones come down from Canada, and as greater and greater chunks of precious wetland have been lost to so-called development, and as black ducks have increasingly hybridized with their more adaptable mallard cousins, the species has been badly threatened. Quite some time ago, then, federal authorities reduced the limit on black duck to one. That's a worthy measure, but as I say, a discouragement: who wants to rise two hours before dawn, put out his spread of decoys, sit unmoving in a brutal cold, only (ideally) to take a single shot, retrieve the decoys, his fingers burning with the chill, and paddle back to the truck?

But I jump-shot this one duck, the one we'll enjoy tonight, late last fall in Maine. The weather had been too rainy and miserable for tromping through dense brush for grouse, so my partner Dave Tobey and I floated Tomah Stream in his canoe, the vast majority of ducks canny enough as not to let us drift up on them, but this one lingering just adequately long.

My wife and I are craving this evening meal. Not to have eaten wild duck for almost two-thirds of our married lives has felt like a deprivation. Not, of course, the sort of deprivation that huge portions of humanity suffer when it comes to nourishment, but one we have registered nonetheless whenever we've spotted a skein of fall blacks in flight overhead or dabbling far ahead of us as we paddle the Connecticut River.

Hunting ducks over decoys is very different from shooting upland birds in New England. Grouse and woodcock inhabit succession forest, the thicker the better, its edges a confoundment of berry-cane, hardhack, popple whip, and so on. Even if one is lucky enough to own a pointing dog who'll pin a ground bird , and I've been multiply so blessed, the instant available to pull the trigger on each of these birds is just that—an instant. One tends to see ducks, on the other hand, well before he can legitimately shoot at them. Often they will circle four or five times before deciding to come into range, and you use your call as expertly as you know how, hoping to draw them over the floating blocks.

As I write this, then, I picture myself, either alone with Topper or one of his predecessors, or with bosom hunting pals, moving only my eyeballs to keep tabs on the flight. But whether consciously or not—and it's surely a conscious thing now—I likewise take in the austere beauty of late autumn, the dark hues of oak leaves clinging stubbornly to riverside trees, the pilasters of mist rising straight as string from the surface; the sun, a pallid disc just breaching Sunday Mountain. I catch the wet of Topper's feet and shins, of the cold mud around us.

Life is more than worthwhile. A shame it should pass so quickly.

I recall from my childhood how Warner Brothers' cat Sylvester would contemplate Tweetie the canary, his vision morphing into the tiny bird dressed like a turkey, those small frilly leggings on either side, the perfectly browned breast steaming on a platter. I confess to similar hallucinations on spying a duck as it approaches my blind, so greatly do I prefer the taste of wild duck to that of any other wild game. Yes, undeniably, a wild duck is one of the hunter's great treats. And yet I am certain that my own yen for the bird has something to do with memories that aren't entirely restricted to taste.

My oldest child's namesake, Creston MacArthur, had a tight little cabin on Third Machias Lake. He and I used to spread decoys off a certain point there, and when we were lucky, we might paddle back to the camp with five or six ducks after a morning's hunt. After the ancient wood-fired cook stove took the chill out of our bones, we'd step outside again to dress the birds, scattering the lovely feathers to the breeze and leaving the insides down in a wetland for the mink and raccoons.

Come evening, we'd kindle the outdoor fire in its ring of stones and, having caged the ducks in a basket broiler, we'd lean the handle against a section of cross-laid road grader blade, which Creston had fetched from somewhere, so that the meat stood in front of the fire and would not char.

You didn't want to cook them too long; the juices still needed to run red when you cut into the meat. Creston and I would sit out there in the dark, eating the ducks with our hands as the few loons left on the lake took up their mournful wails. These were old loons, the young ones already flown to open coastal water. Under the stars of late fall, sharp as razors, we heard one another chewing, groaning, sighing with satisfaction. Now and then a fox might bark along the edge of the marsh, or a loitering bittern, who should have been gone with the young-of-the-year loons, would make that thumping sound for which Creston called the bird "post-driver."

Those meals were more than good. So too the old songs he would sing afterwards, his voice at once rough and tuneful, ones passed down by woodsmen and river-drivers: "The Shores of Gaspereau," "The Lumberjack's Alphabet," and all the rest. I see Creston lift his chin for the high notes, his eyes near popping, his face the very picture of glee.

I've already said elsewhere how I miss him, though he's more than three decades in the grave.

I know there was something primitive about our whole ritual. In spite of that (*because* of that?) there was also something, well, ritual about it too, if you'll spare me some circular logic. Even my own family, seeking as we do to buy local meat and produce whenever possible, having insisted when our children still lived at home that we eat together as a family—even my own family has lost some touch with that ritual basis of consuming our foodstuff. We may not resort to McDonald's or one of its odious equivalents; we don't consume prepared or processed food; but we do seem in a hurry: we need to get fuel into our systems like anyone, but professions and projects seem to tug at us.

Our kids are gone, four of the five with their own careers, the youngest midway through college. Robin and I are apt as not on certain evenings merely to scramble a couple of eggs, make a salad, and sit at the kitchen island for a quarter-hour or so before she heads off to prep a law school class and I, in my retirement, having written most of the day if I've been so moved, to find a suitably challenging crossword puzzle, a televised NBA game, a good novel, or collection of poems. The notion of a meal as a communal, bonding function appears to be fading as quickly as the art of writing letters, even in our rather culturally conservative house.

Tonight's duck will do its part in contravening the anti-ritualism of modern eating habits. My wife is off teaching, and I have spent the better part of two hours getting Annie's sauce just so (though I can't ever get it quite to where she could; I need a little flour to thicken it, as she never did). I will split a passel of oak logs fairly fine, so that they will break down to coals the more quickly (there I go!); I will lay a few strips of paper birch bark into the hearth, arrange adequate kindling on top of it, then tent the hardwood splits over the kindling.

I will remember chill mornings with friends of a lifetime—Landy Bartlett, Joey Olsen, Peter Woerner, Terry Lawson—as we waited for the ducks to give us a peek; I will remember dear dead folks I loved as well: my father, Creston himself. I'll remember the many times around the many twilight blazes.

My history, or at least some glorious moments within it, will burst into mind as the duck's juices burst onto my palate; in fact they have already burst into my thoughts as I write this down. It is perhaps the recollection of wood smoke that slightly burns my eyes until they water a little.

Snowdust

Midmorning yesterday, in an unusually cold and lowery March, I kissed my wife a temporary goodbye where she always follows the trail uphill to complete The Loop, as we call it. Professionally, she was busier than I in my early experience of retirement, and her yen for quick exercise displayed an urgency I had no obligation to share.

She was busier—and a lot faster. We're essentially of identical height, but her thirty-six-inch inseam, as compared to my stubby thirty-one, floats her willowy frame ahead of me at a speed to give me a workout before my intended one begins. I stood a moment to watch her, as ever a glory in my eyes, practically loping uphill. When we embraced, she smelled of cold fresh air. I love that scent.

For her part, she loves repetition, following The Loop every day, savoring its nonpareil view of Moosilauke to our east, the trail's every hollow and ledge her familiar. I prefer exploration, novelty, instinctively getting off-trail as soon as I head out on a ramble, especially during a good winter for snow like this one, when I can pass over the buried brush rather than fighting through it as I must in warmer months. I like that wide whiteness under the canopy, inscribed only by the movements of wild things, whose doings remain a fascination for me, no matter the season.

It wasn't long yesterday morning, in fact, before I came on a clear and perfect narrative: the twin stabs of a fisher exploding at a ragged hole in snow, around which the delicate rusts and grays of grouse feathers and a few little umlauts of blood showed vivid. The bird must have been resting under powder, and couldn't burst out in time to avoid the predator.

There's always something to read out there. So said Donald Chambers, Maine guide, woodsman and lovable friend, and no one has said it better since. I can hear Don's words to this hour, can watch him, short fireplug of a man, making his pronouncement, then sniffing and thumbing his glasses back up his pug nose, his curious habit after passing judgments, which tended to the sage and benign.

Don had an efficiency about him that I always marveled at, vowed to imitate, and by temperament simply couldn't. He would not have understood my urge to meander the way I did yesterday. If there was a place to walk or paddle to, you went directly from here to there. Carrying a pail of water up from the lakeshore to make coffee, you lifted it no more than a sixteenth of an inch over any rock or stump in your way. Why waste energy?

Efficiency—and deliberation, a quality I've also too often lacked. My father, non-plussed himself, once brought him a wind-up clock to which he'd lost the key, for example, and Don sat for a long spell with a ball peen hammer, a flat file and one brass screw until in time he fashioned something workable, as it still is these decades later.

A fellow could cry, I thought. But how in the first place had a fellow gotten here from a tumult of animal sign in snow? He'd certainly taken no unswerving path. The mystery wasn't so deep, though, since my *mind* is never a model of efficiency. Far from it. Yes, there are certain places and people to which it seems almost automatically and directly to go if I leave it alone, as I try to do on these treks, but then it'll be off to who-can-say. If I've proved anything in these pages, that would be it.

There were also living people who called to me as I read the drama of grouse and fisher. Next week, my brother-in-law would have yet another test for cancer. The doctors would check his brain for tumors, as if the colon variety hadn't been enough, and the lung surgery to excise its migratory cells. This was a man I loved like blood family.

Oh, there seemed enough worry to hold me and others, for sure. His mother, a lovely, valiant woman, a living mockery of every stupid mother-in law-joke ever uttered, had fallen the day before out in Colorado. She'd been staying with her youngest of four daughters, happily the one who's a nurse. The tumble caused a mild concussion, but diagnostics revealed something worse: a spine so compromised by osteoporosis as to make it almost indistinguishable from the surrounding soft tissue.

This was a woman who'd been vigorous enough ten years before to hike and paddle with people considerably her junior.

Slightly more than a decade younger myself, I was still able to snowshoe through these two feet of powder and hump my considerable frame along for most of a day after bird dogs, sound enough to wade a fairly bossy trout stream. I was nonetheless subject—for all my denials and exertions—to the same penalties of time as she. Whom would I be fooling to think otherwise?

I wondered as so often what mulish aspect of my nature forced me to give myself little sermons reminding me of my good fortune. A better man and saner would of course have looked at my in-laws' health problems from a better and saner perspective: my wife's brother had barely breached age fifty, and he was where he was. I knew he'd have given all his teeth to be in my snowshoes instead. My mother-in-law would have been gratified by a quarter hour of what I had in amplitude.

And yet the hike I'd planned, up and over Barnet Knoll, then down to an overgrown twitch road to the west, felt just slightly more like a plod now, with that old demon *what's the use* my understated companion, so many of my dearest friends and relatives gone or threatened, and I in what had to be acknowledged as the home stretch.

This hiking was *hard*. Someone of my bulk, snowshoes or no, must post-hole it through such deep powder, and—again, no matter my denials—I couldn't do that as I pushed seventy even as well as I did pushing sixty. I suddenly felt a tart anger at that, but an equal one at my own improvidence.

In autumn, I'd gone to the Internet, as best a techno-Neanderthal could manage, to find a set of longer trail 'shoes than any locally available ones. I needed them for just such a day as this. My three-footers weren't giving me the flotation I needed, and my incipiently stenotic lower back kept complaining about the matter. I'd marked down several brands and designs, any of which would have served me better than what I wore, but I hadn't followed through. Maybe something in me recoiled from mixing cyberspace with the space I'd travel on foot. But now I vowed to see to things that very afternoon, as of course I did not.

When I finally crested Barnet Knoll, I shut down my petty maundering and bitching for a bit to marvel again at wild sign: there were scores of deer cuffings in the red oak stand there. As always, I felt awed and humbled by the life force of the untamed creatures. What skill and avidity went into finding and digging up those acorns! Every day, the whitetails need to find some way to make it through, to discover adequate nourishment. And so do their stalkers.

Evergreen tips around a frozen vernal pool near the mast grove had been trimmed as high as the deer could stand on hind legs. Out on the flat of the pool itself, a pileated woodpecker had showered a pile of square-wrought chips from a moribund hemlock. They flashed like sequins, even beneath a somewhat overcast sky.

A little farther on, the softwoods grew higher and their tops mingled more densely, and whether or not I found them, I knew the tiny golden-crowned kinglets would be busy there, flitting from one tree to another, looking among the shingled cones for enough larvae and grubs, three times their body weight, to see *them* through another day and night.

All this did chasten me, though too mildly. I didn't really know, and never had, what struggle was, at least in its elemental shape, having been so lucky a man in my family, my work as a teacher, my friends and my health. And yet as I reflected on these doings I kept coming back against my will to a notion of animate existence as a persistent scuffle, and ultimately, ineluctably, a losing one.

To go looking for the kinglets, which I had been blessed to see ten or a dozen times, another token of my enviable fortune, struck me less as motive for the time being than habit.

To ratify the pessimistic view, I needed no more than twenty further paces to come across another story in snow: a winter-killed, young-of-the-year deer, everything gone but a patch or two of hide, a single thigh bone, half a spine, and a lower jaw with teeth ripped out. What little the coyotes left had been finished off by ravens and rodents.

The previous night's light snow had sugared all the trees, bough, branch, and bole. Now another shower was floating down. To shove through the thick growth ahead, I figured, would be to dislodge powder from above with every step. Since, bald though I am, I seldom wear a hat, soon enough I'd be feeling the cold stuff direct. I almost short-circuited the hike, but instead, perhaps more in debt to the habitual than even I realized, I cinched my jacket collar tighter, still inwardly whining about one more small misery to endure.

Misery? Endure? Good God.

Thank heaven, the realistic view kept diluting my unmerited self-pity. I'd too often heard fellow higher-academics protest how difficult their lives and work were, and as often silently thought they might try cleaning road kill from a Mississippi highway in summer, say, or tending the lavatories in a hospital for the criminally insane, or simply teaching public high school. And yet here I'd just been grouching that, in my utter leisure, I would have to face a bath or two of clean snow. For all of that, some perverse and inexcusable part of me kept leaning toward a darker account. It tugged at me like a horse at its tether.

There were fairly open woods on the western sidehill before I reached the grander woods. It was midday now, and to my south a winter sun, the color of a Eucharist wafer, faintly glimmered through cloud cover. I had to concede that the cascade of flakes across its face looked lovely.

Thus distracted, I shoulder-brushed a skinny fir, which, prematurely, unexpectedly, did drop a feathery spill onto head and neck. I cursed by instinct, then right away beheld how the finer flakes hovered around me, almost like an aura, that pale sun seeping through it. A net of stars.

And in that instant my region's genius sprang to mind:

Dust of Snow

The way a crow
Shook down on me
The dust of snow
From a hemlock tree

Has given my heart
A change of mood
And saved some part
Of a day I had rued.

Unlike Robert Frost, I hadn't heard or seen a crow, but even if I myself had been the one to shake down snowdust, my day—which, yes, had gone slightly rueful—abruptly turned. It was as though I saw, instantly and thoroughly, my life in its full privilege.

The shimmering torrent seemed a magical powder, mixed by figures from old fairy tale to induce visions of peace and rest. I could have sworn I heard a voice (my own? a breeze's? some god's?) preaching calm.

As so often, a moment also summoned, in a throng, all manner of others like it. It brought back that morning on the flank of Kenyon Hill, just above our yellow house, when my son—now thirty-nine and twice a father himself—touched the back of my neck from his riding pack in a way so delicate it brought on tears. He was only two, and just this side of sleep, but I still feel the fuzzy tip of a mitten stroking a place just under my left ear. I stopped then and stood, gazing at the house through an identical scrim of snow, and felt the sort of peace that comes on a person, if he is lucky, more than once in a lifetime.

It had come on me, I saw, more often than I could reckon, unearned.

To recall that boy on my back was to drift on to each of his four siblings, my oldest daughter thanking me for removing my own mittens, reaching up to clasp her hands, gone cold enough to pain her. Miraculously, she told me, "I love your fingers; they're always nice and warm." I had doubts about my own inner warmth, my perseverant adolescent demons still rampant, and even uglier ones lying in wait down the trail. But from this other trail, an identical snow zigzagging ever so softly through the treetops below what locals called The Hedgehog Den, they were blessedly absent.

And I often hiked with my younger son in the same pack, or one like it, to another place. I'd take him there when he was three or four to shoot with his play bow at imagined game, which he somehow imagined as caribou. The spot was just an old log landing, but we named it Caribou Country.

After he'd taken a score or so of shots, some pretty good at that, I hefted him again, turned onto the downhill route homeward, and began jogging, in a way knees and back would prohibit today, singing a song that began, "I bought a mule, he's such a fool/ That he never paid no heed." I'd learned the song from one of the Maine woodsmen who've so shaped my life.

As I write this, I see Creston MacArthur inside his Third Lake camp, having swallowed a belt or two of something amber, veins pushing out in his neck as he chants the refrain:

> *Go 'long mule,*
> *Don't you roll them eyes!*
> *You can change a fool*
> *But a goldang mule*
> *Am a mule until he dies.*

The lake is buckling outdoors; it's getting on mid-March, like today. The stove glows crimson, warming the place so that ice dams thaw and drip from the eaves. There's that smell of must and man and woodfire I'll always treasure. *I'd* be the fool to wish myself anywhere else.

On the later day I recalled, my second son sang Creston's tune with me for a hundred feet or so. Then he stopped mid-breath, even before we got to the refrain. I slowed to a walk, recognizing that he was deep in slumber, which likely meant he'd dropped the small plastic bow behind us. Without checking, I hiked back up the trail a short distance, and sure enough, there it lay, glowing red as an exhausted star in the snow.

I stooped and fetched the puny weapon, then looked out across the valley from Stonehouse Mountain. Everything so beautiful. Why hadn't I been noticing this right along? Same snow, same peace, same sense of possibility and gratitude.

I couldn't stop now. I thought back to the middle daughter as we descended another flank of the same mountain, her warmth piercing through the pack and my two layers of clothing. She had been sleeping almost from the moment we left the house, yet all along had been so profoundly *there*. Below me, under a gnarled and woodpecker-ravaged beech tree, my bird dog Bessie stood stock still, as if she pointed some phantom woodcock. But no: she was merely gazing at her master, who stood stock still himself in that long moment, mumbling something related to hosanna, amazed not least that so noble an animal was thus concerned with *him* of all people!

And finally, twenty years gone now, the last child, my namesake, removing her glove and waving her pudgy fist through the same peaceful, frigid flurry, chanting a little nonce ditty whose words I've forgotten. But words weren't the main thing here. Sometimes they aren't. I stooped to pluck the mitten from a drift and slipped it back on.

Finally—and all this, I suspect, in less than a minute—I went back even farther in time to a solo descent of Dougherty Ridge in Maine, where snowshoe hare, white as flakes themselves, kept flitting back and forth across the ancient logging road I followed. That they should keep bursting out of the brush like that, displaying themselves to a man who in those days killed fifty or so a season . . . well, it seemed apparitional, as by God it was.

Hosanna indeed.

My self-preoccupation, whenever it rears its head, is unforgivable, and, if I think matters through, I know that. It will forevermore be a mystery to me why I must feel my way out of such funk, or more specifically, remember my way out. At too long last, not merely the benisons of my present life but older ones as well will at length prevail over sorrow at natural loss.

That the last of our children was out of the house now must surely have had something to do with that vague inner sorrow I took into the woods yesterday. And yet surely the most important aspect of my part in raising all five involved their capacity to distract me from—me.

So I hoped it would be with my children's children. And so it has been. Not that I'd begin to claim I have continuously been so distracted. I will forever regret any moments I lived in unwitting disregard of the children's cravings and passions and fears, of those of their mothers, of anyone's beyond that fetid thing, my puling self.

For all that, if I ever complained (and what parent doesn't?) about the frequent chorishness of parenthood, even at my worst I knew deep inside that the end validated the busywork, that in fact it wasn't busywork at all. And the moments I'd recalled, in winter, in snow, children on my back both literally and metaphorically, would sustain me if nothing else did, if I could only be moved, despite myself, to summon them, just as I'd lately done on Barnet Knoll.

All it took was a little snow.

Standing there a day ago, I knew that a warm house awaited, but I lingered, looking up now, willy-nilly, to see Earl Bonness ahead of me, wearing the elegant snowshoes he'd wrought in that little red shop. Earl was a man who knew pain much more than most of us ever do, and certainly more than I.

There was the sudden, incomprehensible death of his daughter at sixteen, dropped to the floor in the middle of a basketball game. His courageous younger son Alan, cursed with cystic fibrosis, worked himself literally off his feet, determined to do a job right, tumbling behind a push lawnmower or collapsing under an armful of stove wood, until he finally fell for good in his early forties. There was the catastrophic death by gunshot of his grandson Tommy, which Earl insisted until his own death was no suicide but was after all still death, a boy whom, for family reasons, he and his wife Tecky had raised.

Earl wore pain on his face and in his matchless basso voice, but he never went further in my company than to say, "Memories can bear down on you."

Indeed they can. But they can buoy as well. As in mind I scanned from Earl to Donald, from Donald to George, from George to Creston, from Creston to Carter, from Carter to Annie, from Annie to Ada, and on and on, beholding their faces with an inner eye, a kind of enlightenment fell on me like the snow I'd lately jostled.

What was it I'd so treasured in each and all? The capacity, precisely, to joy in how and where and what they lived. Most had known hard times and hard work that I couldn't conceive, but they were sturdy, often even jolly, which was to say they valued their lives on life's terms.

I heard the voice of George just then, after I asked him how he'd stood the crushing labor of his young manhood: piecework, out by lantern in the morning, back the same way at night. *You took pride in your work,* he told me. *And if you couldn't fix something, you let it be.*

My principal labor was a luxury, even an embarrassment, compared. It was no more than the ongoing effort truly to reckon what a bounty this life, both active and reflective, had offered, and then to write as much of it down as I could.

I thought, you'd better hope you can change a fool.

All this from a small, bright dust of snow.

I'd had to hike a little more strenuously than I'd forecast, breaking trail to where I stood in reminiscence; even I knew it might be more than I'd bargain for to pursue the route I originally intended. To hell with pride, I decided, swinging south, homeward, snaking through the woods as best I could, helped on my way by the long decline.

In a quarter of an hour or so, I stepped onto a white space that stretched west to east out of sight. I gaped, having thought in decades of searching through these three hundred–odd acres I knew their every inch. Yet here I was on an old tote road I'd never seen! Had I missed it in the warm months because vegetation grew thick across it? I didn't think so. Years of bushwhacking had made me adept at tracing trails that most might never notice.

I knew which way the house lay. I was not lost, not even, as those old woodsmen said, turned around. But everything in every direction looked brand new to me, the untouched belt of snow a palette for memory and imagination both. And was that a tiny dash of olive-gray in my eye's corner in the almost equally tiny gap between two tall spruces? Had my kinglets come?

Had I been here before or not, and what did *here* mean anymore?

This surely seemed a new path, and its untouched whiteness provided the old inducement to walk it in one direction or the other. If there were literal, geographical places in my own back woods that I hadn't explored, what other sorts of exploration had I failed to make?

Yes, I could head either way and see what was what. Neither way pointing home, though, I'd mark the ghost road in mind, and save it for a later day.

Photograph by Steve Takach

Don Chambers (right) and hunting companion Hazen Bagley.

About the Author

Sydney Lea is an American poet, novelist, essayist, editor, and professor, who is currently the Poet Laureate of Vermont. He has taught at Dartmouth College, Yale University, Wesleyan University, Vermont College, Middlebury College, Franklin College, and the National Hungarian University. He founded *New England Review* in 1977 and edited it until 1989. His stories, poems, essays and criticism have appeared in *The New Yorker, The Atlantic, The New Republic, The New York Times, Sports Illustrated* and many others, as well as in more than forty anthologies. He lives in Newbury, Vermont.